Pour Me Some ~~Whine~~ Wine!

A Toast to the Mama Sisterhood!

Katrina (Trina) Epp & Leah Speer

CHANGING LIVES PRESS

CHANGING LIVES PRESS
P.O. Box 140189
Howard Beach, NY 11414
www.changinglivespress.com

Library of Congress Cataloging-in-Publication Data is available through the Library of Congress.

ISBN: 978-0-9904396-3-9

Cover design by Michael Short
Interior layout by Gary A. Rosenberg • www.thebookcouple.com

Printed in the United States of America

10   9   8   7   6   5   4   3   2

CONTENTS

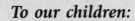

To our children:
You brighten our lives each and every single day!
Because of our journey together, from sleepless
nights and tantrums to cuddles and laughter, you
inspired us to write this book—not to mention
enjoy that glass of wine at the day's end.

Acknowledgments

First, we would like to thank Michele Matrisciani. Girl, you are awesome! We feel so blessed to have met you at the beginning of our journey and that you saw the potential of our idea and helped us develop it into a book. Your passion for it and insight into the publishing world made you a wonderful confidant and invaluable guide. We also credit your brilliant writing and sales skills for where we are today. We've enjoyed working with you every minute—and consider you a friend.

We offer many thanks to Francesca Minerva and Marie Timell, our witty publisher and editor, for your vision and hard work. Francesca: thank you for seeing the potential of a book that celebrates mothers and wine—a complimentary pair. Thank you Marie, you taught us so much with your editing skills, making for an exciting collaboration. We are thrilled that, together, we delivered what *Pour Me Some Wine* was really meant to be.

We would also like to thank those individuals who volunteered their stories and experiences. A toast to you Mama Sisters!

Trina adds:

I must thank my brilliant and savvy writing partner, Leah Speer. If it weren't for you, this book would not be possible! You are my other half in this and, together, we make quite the pair. Thanks for being an amazing business partner and friend.

To my babies, Callie and Clay—without you, I wouldn't have been given the utmost gift of being a mother and therefore would not be the woman I am today, with the drive to be everything for your two beautiful little souls. I am so proud of you both and look forward to seeing what awesome little individuals you will each become.

To the family and friends who supported me on this journey and in the countless celebrations that have followed each tiny step of success—I love you and couldn't have done this without you either.

And last, but most certainly not least—to *wine*. I dearly love you! And I look forward to our journey of learning, relaxation, and experimentation over the next many, many years.

Leah adds:

Trina, nobody could have written our story. It's far too unique and, simply, incredible. Through the years, I've found an amazing writing partner and business cohort in you, but most importantly I've found a great friend. This book just wouldn't be what it is without your passion and drive. I truly can't wait to finally share a bottle *or two* of wine with you!

This brings me to you, dearest wine. I have appreciated you ever more and have missed you so throughout this current pregnancy. I look forward to reuniting with you for a lifetime of adventures beginning again this fall.

I am forever thankful to my coterie of supporters, who, from the beginning urged me to follow my dreams. From Nashville to New York City; San Diego to Santa Rosa Beach, each of you have taught me what true friendship is and how a true mom's night out is not complete without good friends and good wine.

My mother, Carole Bellacera, deserves special thanks for passing on her passion for writing and for embodying the true nature of never, ever giving up. And it is thanks to my father, Frank Bellacera, that I was raised with a sense of humor—something I couldn't live without. And thank you to my little brother, Stephen Bellacera, for his unwavering encouragement.

I thank my husband, who not only contributed to some of this material, but has supported me and joined me in my appreciation for a glass of good wine after settling a house full of children into beautiful sleep.

Most importantly, I thank Luke and Zealand who over the past six years have provided me with endless inspiration for stories about the essence of motherhood, a part of my life I would never trade. Being your mom has been a dream come true.

Introduction

*p*our *Me Some Wine* is dedicated to our mama sisterhood. It reflects our own journey as moms and as "mommoisseurs," or wine enthusiasts who happen to also be fabulous mothers. Combining stories on a wide range of topics with wine recommendations, *Pour Me Some Wine* is our offer of support to our fellow moms. In it we express many of the emotions that most of us experience day-to-day, from mom guilt to celebration. Perhaps you just want to connect to other moms for a minute, but your go-to girls are unavailable. In this book, you are sure to find a story that reflects your experience at any given time to nourish and support you. You'll also find a wine recommendation that is the perfect pairing for when you need to take a few moments for yourself to kick back and relax. Do you want to become a mommoisseur too? Later we share how you can learn more about wine and join our mama sisterhood of connoisseurs. Or, do you just want a suggestion for a good wine for yourself, to share, or for entertaining? Then consider this to be a compendium of ideas for ensuring that, when the circumstances are right, you'll enjoy a great glass of wine.

The day we become moms is a defining moment for us.

Almost immediately, our priorities and lives change irrevocably as our focus shifts away from ourselves and onto our families. But it's all worth it because raising a child is the most beautiful gift in the world. Yet motherhood can also be an emotional and sometimes lonely journey, one becoming increasingly complex in the 21st century. Fortunately, women have always supported each other. And when it comes to motherhood, this support is critical. By sharing our experiences, our sorrows, and our joys, we help each other in the transformational work of being a mom.

More often than not, it is by telling our stories that we moms nurture each other, leaning on one another for support and reassurance, knowing that none of us is perfect and we're all in this crazy race together. Sometimes, there is nothing more valuable than talking with other moms during playdates or at the park. There often isn't anything more healing or a better reality check than a long chat with a girlfriend. And how crucial isn't a girls' night out once in a while? Because motherhood is full of emotional ups and downs, we need other mothers to laugh at the ridiculousness of life and to share with pride our children's red-letter days with us.

Everyone is busy today. There is a lot of talk about "work/life balance." Yet mothers have been doing a balancing act since the beginning of time. We give ourselves over to motherhood, but that doesn't mean we stop being people with our own needs, even though often they are put on hold. That's why we moms need both our friends as well as me-time to stay sane. It's crucial for us to have a few things for ourselves: a bubble bath, a yoga class, a morning of quiet with a favorite book or catching up on the news of the world—or, in our case, a glass of wine, whether to soothe jangled nerves or simply to celebrate.

As wine lovers, we have learned that wine can be an adventure all its own—and all our own. And we're not talking about

Is It Okay for Moms to Drink?

Yes, but it's important to drink responsibly. The United States Department of Agriculture (USDA) considers moderate drinking to be a glass of wine a day. While we enjoy wine, our commitment to being loving parents and role models for our children always comes first. You may not choose to drink in front of your kids, but if you do, it's always best to show them that you can enjoy a drink now and then without needing it or wanting more. If you start to notice that you are drinking too often or too much, it may be time to seek some support.

Also, the American Congress of Obstetricians and Gynecologists (ACOG) recommends abstaining from drinking alcohol of any kind while pregnant. We like to stick with what the experts say. The main reason they recommend abstention is that nobody knows what the "safe limit" for drinking alcohol during pregnancy really is. Furthermore, this safe limit may vary from woman to woman and fetus to fetus. So the majority of women choose not to drink at all during pregnancy. Besides, you'll make it through your pregnancy soon enough and can celebrate the birth of your baby with your favorite glass of red or white.

This leads us to the discussion of having a glass of wine while you're breast-feeding. The decision to breast-feed is a personal one. As a new mom, you deserve support no matter how you decide to feed your baby. The American Academy of Pediatrics (AAP) recommends that babies be exclusively breast-fed, with no supplements, for the first six months of life. They also advise that breast-feeding continue for 12 months or longer if mutually desired. So, 9 months being pregnant plus 12 months of nursing equals 21 months without wine. Now that's a long time to go without wine!

The good news is you don't have to totally abstain those months you're nursing. There are a couple of ways to enjoy that glass of wine while you're breast-feeding. First, as long as the alcohol is in your blood stream, it will be in your breast milk. So if you drink, your body must process and clear the alcohol before it is safe to breast-feed. The more alcohol the longer it takes. The time it takes to process one glass of wine is about two hours. (Note: though people talk about the "pump and dump"—expressing your contaminated breast milk to throw it away—this does not clear alcohol from your system any faster. It will still take at least two hours before you can breast-feed again.)

With this understanding you can do a couple of things. The first is to time having a glass right after a feeding or during one of your baby's longer stretches of sleep so that your baby won't need to nurse for a few hours. In this way, your body can process and clear the alcohol. Second, and our personal-favorite option, is to pump ahead of time, storing the milk in the refrigerator, to feed you baby with when you've had a glass of wine. This way, you can imbibe and feel great knowing your baby still gets the benefit of your nutritious breast milk—you're not throwing away your liquid gold.

One useful tool during breast-feeding is a home test called Milkscreen. It tests and measures the amount of alcohol in breast milk so it takes away any guesswork about whether alcohol is still in your system. You simply dip the paper stick in the milk and the testing strip analyzes the milk's alcohol content. Brilliant!

chugging a glass out of frustration or angst. Contrary to what some seem to believe—that wine drinking should be taboo for moms—we've found that it can be an exciting sensory education. In the pages that follow, we share our experiences as moms as well as what we have learned as wine enthusiasts—

because being a mom and a mommoisseur are not mutually exclusive.

Our Journey with Wine

Over the years, we went from college-age gals drinking Boones Farm to ladies with jobs splurging on Kendall Jackson or even better—Carlo Rossi. Back in those days we couldn't afford much and wine-tasting events seemed like the "classy" next step for us 21st-century ladies. Our knowledge grew as we matured into women who actually attended dinner parties instead of just clubs. The next best thing: wine bars. We didn't even notice as Napa crept to the top of the vacation bucket list—eclipsing spring break in Cancun. We were growing up and starting to learn what it truly means to enjoy the finer things in life. The best part is that we're still learning.

As we became more wine oriented, we discovered a true passion for it as we tried tasting, sampling, and pairing. When we went out, we began to switch our drink orders from the usual vodka tonic or fruity martini to wines we didn't know. Then we started paying attention to pairing wine with dinner. In restaurants, we'd eagerly ask the waiter for suggestions about the correct pairings with the menu items. When we cooked, we began to revel in paying attention to the aromas of the food and the tastes and flavors that the wine brought out, discovering for example, how well a deep, red blend complemented a flavorful juicy steak. Soon we began to notice how wine paired with mood. It became clear that whites pair well with happier, upbeat moods, especially the bubbly blends for celebrations. Meanwhile, we came to appreciate how soothing, almost healing, some reds can be after a long day—for example, a Chianti goes perfectly with a relaxing (once-quiet) bubble bath.

Then everything changed. We became mothers. There was nothing more important than those tiny adorable little humans that we'd so looked forward to meeting. Before there was time to adjust, we'd had more children and our families grew. We barely had time to notice that suddenly the fun nights out at tastings and wine bars, the dinner parties where everyone brought a different bottle to try, and those pampering moments alone with a glass were now gone. They'd been squelched by dirty diapers, long sleepless nights, crying and temper tantrums, and running from one place to another, trying to balance a crazy schedule and run a busy household. *Wine who?* We were lucky if we fit in a shower most of the time.

As the kids grew, we started to realize that we needed part of that old life back. We missed relishing a wonderful, relaxing glass of wine with girlfriends, trying out different flavors as we cooked, or simply taking the time to expand our knowledge of such a beautiful and wonderful thing.

We decided that we can still have those times and that it's okay to take a few moments here and there to try new wines and continue to experience and learn about wine. We bought some books such as *The Everything Guide to Wine* because we wanted to take our indulgence to a new level of understanding. This led to spending hours doing research online, attending some wine tastings again, and turning to some of our savvy friends who paired wine with cheese and appetizers with flair. We also picked the brains of the experts at local wine shops.

As our education progressed, we learned to try to pair wines with our moods or emotions and to make wine recommendations to other mothers. We would share what we knew about wine the same way we shared our experiences as moms.

We slowly morphed from simply being lovers of wine to proud mommoisseurs.

The Story of Our Friendship

Because we lived in two different parts of the country, our friendship was an unlikely one—yet one that was clearly meant to be. It all started when Trina enrolled in a writing class offered by Leah's mom, Carole Bellacera, and became close to her almost immediately. Carole would often talk about her daughter Leah, how we were similar in age, and also how we had children around the same age. Once we contacted each other, we quickly learned how much we had to talk about: our lives as moms, our shared loved of writing—and our interest in wine. Our connection proved to us how fate can be utterly, unexpectedly wonderful—and that it has the ability to totally change your life.

As we shared our experiences as moms and wine lovers, it wasn't long before we knew we wanted to write this book. It was an exciting time for us as we set to work on making it a reality. We both had two young children and were crazy busy taking care of our families and managing our hectic schedules as well as work. But once this book had sparked a passion and drive in us, the busyness of the days no longer mattered. We stayed up, far past bedtime, writing. And then, early in the morning, we were writing. We wrote with babies bouncing on our laps and toddlers tapping on our keyboards. And in between, we tried and tested wines. *Pour Me Some Wine* was born—and with it an unbreakable bond of friendship as well.

ABOUT THE BOOK

Just as moms all over the world share their stories with one another, in *Pour Me Some Wine* we offer you our stories as well as those of other mothers. We want readers to not only experience the comfort we've found in our friendship and storytelling but also the blissful moments of pampering yourself with the perfect glass of wine, selected for the perfect moment.

There is a common thread that weaves through all of the stories in the book and, we believe, the lives of most of us: the sometimes confusing welter of emotions that come with being a mom. So each chapter in the book includes stories that reflect those feelings. What is our most constant companion? Guilt. How often don't we feel frustrated, overwhelmed and stressed out? And then there are all the worries and fears that we go through as well as the heartbreaks, some often unforeseen. Throughout it all we are growing and learning about ourselves, our choices, and our mistakes. One thing we may learn is that other adults, including our husbands, sometimes pose unique challenges that we may not be in the mood to deal with. And, of course, there are stories full of gratitude, hope, and celebration. Whenever you need a pick-me-up, think about how you are feeling, turn to the chapter that describes it, and read a few of the stories. We hope they will offer the relief of knowing that *we've all been there* and make you realize that *you are not alone.*

After each story we suggest a wine ("DARE TO PAIR"), specifically selected for its flavor, aroma, and how it pairs with the mood of the story. As we have discovered, pairing wine is not just about food, it's about making wine the perfect accompaniment to our lives. It's the perfect cab to pair with the inevitable sadness in dropping our children off at school for the first time. And it's the ideal floral and fruity Moscato to go with the giggles over the embarrassing incident at the pediatrician's. There's the robust red blend to sip as we reflect on the hard times and the Chardonnay to celebrate whatever is going right or to toast the latest hard-won milestone.

If you are learning to share our love of wine with us (for some tips on how to get started or to progress in what you already know see the special section that follows) or just want to occasionally enjoy a good wine, try the wines we've selected and savor them in a quiet moment as you read the stories. Collectively, think of these wines as being your own private wine cellar. They can be a wonderful addition to your wine education, or if you aren't interested in learning about wine, a shortcut to picking the perfect wine for whatever occasion brought you to our book. At the back of the book is an index of our wine recommendations, organized by red or white, which enables you to select a good wine quickly and easily. No matter the mood or emotion, we have a wonderful, tasty wine pairing to match.

Whether or not you read the book straight through from cover to cover, flip through it, select a chapter based on how you're feeling, or plan to expand your interest in wine, it is our wish that the stories and the suggested wines in *Pour Me Some Wine* both support and nourish you. We hope that you will find here a reflection of our friendship, our love of motherhood—and our proud love of being mommoisseurs.

Becoming a Mommoisseur

Become mommoisseurs with us! Make wine an event and pamper yourself, girl. Try a few of the wines we suggest and find comfort in the stories that we offer from moms who have been right where you are now. Don't stop being a first-class wine lover just because you have babies. Ladies, it's a not-so-new, yet hip, era for us wine lovers, *moms*.

You can begin or continue your education right at home. Through various online videos, books or through a local wine-store event, learn the basics of wine tasting from the type of glasses to use to the five "S" steps: see, swirl, smell, sip, savor.

Next buy a few different bottles of reasonably priced wines, paying attention to buy different varietals, for example, a Merlot, a Chianti, and a Riesling. Where wine is available for purchase will depend on what state you live in. (If you live in a dry county, we suggest moving. Yes, seriously.) Another way to begin is to visit your local wine shop and have the staff recommend a couple of good starter bottles within your budget. Take the bottles home, read the labels, research the bottles online, and learn all you can about those specific wines—in other words, become at one with your wine. In this way, you will figure out which grape varieties you like.

When things at home have quieted down, grab a good book, start a bath, and pour a glass of one of your recent purchases. Sit back for thirty minutes, reading and enjoying the wine in the silence. When you sniff it what aromas, good or bad, do you sense? Notice the taste or aftertaste. Does it feel good on your palate? Finally, notice how the traditional third of a glass used for tastings makes you feel. Has your mood changed at all? When we first began to enjoy wine this way, we could hear the kids screaming beyond the bedroom. But since they were being carefully watched, I could disregard it. We kept at it, determined to have that bit of time to ourselves. Of course, you don't have to sit in the tub every time you try a new wine, but it is important to have a little peace and quiet.

Once you've learned your go-to favorites by varietal, further expand your knowledge base by learning about the regions where those grapes are grown. For instance, if you learn that Cabernet Sauvignon is one of your favorites, sample cabs from different regions such as Bordeaux in France or from the Napa and Sonoma Valleys in California. Once you have sampled and noted several, you'll begin to get a feel for what area produces a richer, heavier, lighter, more savory, or fruity grape.

Wine tasting doesn't have to happen at the winery. Take twenty minutes during naptime, or after bedtime, or whenever it is you get the chance. But, just as you savor a wine slowly, sip by sip, take your time as you progress in wine appreciation. Continue your wine education and feed that love for the sake of the knowledge of something so wonderful. Most of all, let it be something that is all yours as you pamper yourself.

Many wine shops have free tastings, so on your monthly girls' night out have everyone go to a tasting before you go out to dinner. Try to begin with an "all-white" or "all-red" tasting in the beginning. Organize monthly tastings with a theme at your home. Invite friends over and have everyone bring their favorite white wine. Or, have everyone bring a bottle from a different region (assign each person a place so nobody doubles up).

Then start to learn about wine pairing, or what wine matches what food best. This is an art in itself. Whether cooking at home or going out, notice how the wine pairs with the meal. The key here is to try matching at least one taste or smell in the wine to what you are cooking. If you are eating in a restaurant and it pairs a wine you've never had with the meal you've ordered, go for it. Let it be another wine adventure.

Throughout all your wine experiences, jot down the names of all the wines you try in a notebook and keep track of your tasting notes. Better yet, go to CellarTracker.com and start an account. There you can track the wines you've purchased, your notes, and even see other members' comments on the wine you're trying. They even have an app for your iPhone so you can easily record your notes as you relax on the couch or in bed with your glass of vino.

Make an effort to splurge on holidays, and for Super Bowls, Oscar parties, wedding anniversaries, your children's birthdays etc. But note that Valentine's Day deserves the best. Spend an extra 10 dollars on a new wine. Don't feel guilty. Many men enjoy a round of golf on the weekends that can cost four times what one decent bottle will cost you. Don't be shy!

Are the grandparents available to watch the kids? For some romance as well as education, spend the weekend with your lover at a bed-and-breakfast near a winery. Now *really* pair your wine and see how it complements the occasion.

CHAPTER 1

Guilty

*A*s mothers, wives, sisters, friends, daughters, employees, and bosses (not necessarily in that order), we all know about guilt. It seems to be our constant companion—so it's no surprise that "Guilty" is the first chapter of the book.

When that negative inner voice begins to beat you up—take a moment to relate to the stories in this chapter. You'll find comfort in knowing you're *not* alone. And as you treat yourself to one of the recommended wines and gain perspective, you may just feel encouraged to embrace your imperfections and let go of mommy guilt.

I Feel Guilty No Matter What I Do!

"Stay at home or work. It really doesn't matter *what* you do. You'll find a way to feel guilty about something either way. You just have to do what feels right for you and what works best for your family." So explained a wise, dear friend of mine. As we chatted on the phone, I stared out at Seattle's Space Needle from my luxurious, very quiet (aah, I remember quiet) hotel room, rubbing my almost eight-months-pregnant belly.

At the time, I wanted nothing more than to be a stay-at-home mom. It had been my dream, even after ten years of exciting business trips and extravagant meals at the best restaurants across the country. But there didn't seem to be a way to make two mortgages work on one salary. So it made me feel better about my decision to be a working mom when my old friend, a working mom who seems to do motherhood seamlessly, told me that *all* moms feel guilty about something some of the time.

Three years and two toddlers later, as a work-at-home-mom, I now know this to be true. No matter what you try to do right for your family or your children (*or yourself*), guilt will sneak its way in. Here are just some of the ways guilty-mom syndrome kicks in.

The Working Mom

HER EARLY MORNING THOUGHTS: Today, I'm going to be the best mom ever! I'm going to work hard to teach my kids how successful you can be in life, while also making money so we can have what we need to be comfortable, and, hey, even a Disney Vacation or two.

HER GUILT: I should be home with my kids—doing crafts, flipping through Sight Words Flash Cards, taking them to the park, making them a healthy, home-cooked lunch and kissing them at nap time.

The Stay-at-Home Mom

HER EARLY MORNING THOUGHTS: Today, I'm going to be the best mom ever! I'm going to spend hours in one-on-one time with my children, giving them love and affection, teaching them about the world and making a craft out of autumn leaves and paint. We'll run around the house, laughing the day away. I will make them a healthy, home-cooked lunch before I kiss them at nap time.

HER GUILT: I don't have time to cook these kids a healthy, home-cooked lunch—there are toys all over the place, paint all over the table and chairs, and I can't even get them to sit still for one minute to do our flash cards. What if I'm playing with them too much and they don't learn how to play independently? I feel so guilty for wanting it to be nap time!

The Work-at-Home Mom

HER EARLY MORNING THOUGHTS: Today, I'm going to be the best mom ever! I'm going to balance playing with my kiddos and working on my business plan. I'll take time to prepare a healthy, home-cooked lunch and snuggle with them before their two-hour nap. During nap time, I'll get in a few solid hours of work. Afterwards I'll let them run around during a park playdate.

HER GUILT: I just spent thirty minutes playing doctor and being locked up in jail. I painted with them earlier today. We're going to the playground after nap time. Yet, I still feel bad about stealing a few minutes to work on my laptop. Sometimes I can get up to 15 minutes in; the rest of the time I feel like I'm neglecting them. I swear they would be happier in preschool, learning and playing with other kids. The day is ticking by; and all I want is to get some work done. Even if I feel guilty about it, I'll just have to settle for a SpaghettiOs® lunch and some TV time in the afternoon if that's what it takes for me to make some progress writing.

So there it is moms—guilt at its finest. You can try to do the right thing to be the best mom ever, but there is always a flip side. You're either doing too much or too little. But don't forget all you do right: light up when your child walks into a room; your rapt attention when he is holding that invisible microphone and shaking his groove thing for his favorite audience; the way you hold him tight at night reading a bedtime story; and each kiss and whispered "I love you" you give. Instead of getting swept up in all the things we can't do or control, let the simple, beautiful moments—the ones that *really* matter—slay the guilt. It will always be there. Let love triumph.

DARE TO PAIR

Whether you stay at home or work, you deserve a relaxing moment now and then. When you feel the pressure of guilt start to build, we suggest putting on some Sinatra, accompanied by a glass of **Two Rivers' Riesling**. With fresh aromas and flavors of peach, green apple, and honeydew, this wine is sure to keep the positive energy abundantly flowing.

Ashamed at How Shallow I Was

"Well, what if we have a boy?" My husband asked one day.

Pondering this for only a second, I decided: not possible! What do you do with a boy? They could only be a nightmare of boogers, burping, and other disgusting behaviors. Nope, I was going to have a girl!

I had never wanted children, *necessarily*. As selfish and vain as I was, my body was important to me, and there wasn't anything that could make me want to ruin it the way I'd imagined many mothers did by having children.

And I recoiled at the thought of the poopy diapers, the snotty noses, and the sleepless nights—none of it sounded appealing to me. So you can only imagine my lack of glee when my husband announced that he was ready to have a baby. Of course, while I think we all compromise with our spouses on one thing or another, this was just a little too big to swallow.

After a ton of coaxing from him and, of course, from both of our families, I began to consider it. Slowly, I adapted to the idea by picturing myself curling my future daughter's hair, shopping for her clothes, and browsing a bookstore with her. In fact, I started to see that we could do everything together. Suddenly, having a baby seemed a whole lot more reasonable.

Studying the Internet for hours, I researched how to ensure that I'd have a girl. Nothing was too far-fetched for me, from studying family trees to sex positions to even using a system based on the Chinese calendar to predict the sex of your baby. I was going to do whatever it took. So I did it all, all the tips, all the advice. When I got pregnant on the first try, I could already feel the itch to start buying clothes—*pink* clothes.

Extremely anxious, I almost didn't make it to 20 weeks, but thankfully, the day of the ultrasound finally came. I'll never forget the tears that fell, and continued to fall, after I found out I was having a boy. "Can you check again?" I kept asking my doctor.

Today, I'm ashamed to admit that I didn't speak to my husband for days; and, as foolish as it sounds now, for a moment, I didn't even want the baby. I understand why people were annoyed with me and thought my bitterness was ridiculous considering how many women can't get pregnant and would do anything to have my little boy. Back then, I didn't care; I was enveloped in my own pity party.

You see, I'd always been a planner. Everything was planned to a tee. From my schedule to my life, I knew exactly what would happen next. Thinking about it now, I'm pretty sure the lack of control is what bothered me more than not having the little girl I'd dreamed of.

When I went into labor, I hardly knew it. A few pains and Nick was here. It was as though my small, thin body was made just for *this*—for having babies. When my eyes locked on Nick's, I knew. I loved him more than life itself; and the thought of never having had him nearly suffocated me right then and there.

How stupid I'd been! How selfish! This was driven home again and again each day as I watched him grow and we created memories together.

DARE TO PAIR

We've all looked at our children in ways that, on a better day, we are a bit ashamed of. But sometimes fate just sends us a doozy like when you've begged for a little girl, yet now you're buying boring blue jeans and T-shirts instead of an array of little pink dresses and bows. Before you start feeling bad about yourself or throwing up your middle finger at fate in rage, get some perspective by taking a time-out and purchasing a bottle of this medium-bodied **Twisted Old Vine Zinfandel**. The aromas of black cherry, red currant, and blackberry bramble are just the right fit for your black mood. Also, just as the flavors of ripe fruit and dark pepper move stealthily through the palate, as you slowly calm down, you will begin to see and maybe even accept that it all may have been your best destiny.

Because I'd Rather Work Doesn't Make Me a Terrible Mom

Nobody has ever said that balancing being a mommy with working full-time is easy. Nor do they say being a stay-at-home mommy is easy either. In the last three years, I've done both; and neither one is very easy, to be honest.

After working full-time the entire six years I'd been a mom, I quit my successful career as an account executive to stay at home with my two children and write my first book. I was super excited—my house would always be clean! I would have time to play and color with the kids as well as write and have time to myself too. I'd no longer be commuting 30 miles to work so obviously I'd get more sleep. Overall, I was confident my lifestyle would become more well-rounded and satisfying.

Oh, how little did I know back then! As soon as I had my last day at work, I watched my life become a wreck. Because I didn't have a schedule or anywhere to be, I overslept, losing the first hour or two of my day. Excited that their mom was home with them, the kids rarely napped. I spent all day doing dishes, cooking, and getting snacks, not to mention laundry and other motherly duties. *Write?* Heck I didn't have time to shower half the time, let alone write. How the hell had I worked a forty-hour-a-week job before? I couldn't get done even a fraction of the stuff I'd gotten done when I worked. I felt deflated.

It took time, but I eventually realized that those eight hours I'd previously worked out of the home were time for *me.* I had had a full lunch hour to myself, plus breaks to pay bills and make phone calls, which I no longer had. I now had a child attached to my hip 24/7, with no time for lunch with friends or even time to think. It was exhausting! It was *me* who needed a nap now. Not to mention that I no longer had the freedom to spend money at will the way I'd had before. Counting on someone else to take care of me financially was hard to accept, especially after being the independent woman I'd always prided myself on being.

After less than a year at home, I realized I needed to go back to work—for my own sanity's sake if not for the financial freedom. I needed the set schedule, the hours away, for myself, the challenge of working, and the pride and self-satisfaction work gave me. Once I started interviewing, I found that, in those eight months at home, I'd lost myself.

I did feel guilty about wanting to go back to work. What mom wants to work and be away from her kids? But the truth is: I'd failed as a stay-at-home mom. After being back at work now for more than a year, I'm a better mom. With a schedule, I'm more disciplined and happier when I'm home, which is good for my kids. Financially, I can now offer them more, such as vacations, classes, and things I couldn't have before. Plus, I'm showing my children how to be successful and independent.

DARE TO PAIR

With its flavors of peach, apricot nectar, green melon, pear, and spicy vanilla, Caymus Vineyards' **Conundrum White** is for all the mommies out there who struggle with the constant battle between staying at home or working. This robust white blend with green apple, tangerine, and honeysuckle blossom aromas is sure to calm the welter of feelings created by this common quandary.

Just as each one of us is unique as a woman, every mom is different. Some are born and bred to have the patience and know-how to stay at home full-time to mother their babies. Some, like me, are built for work and juggling career and motherhood. No matter which type of mom you are, embrace it and revel in it. Because, it's when we are at our personal best that we can be the best role models and providers for our children.

It's Not a Failure if You Make a Decision to Better Your Life

At 30, I made a decision that I wasn't going to trade in happiness for a mediocre or average life. I decided to have the life I truly wanted, even if it meant being called selfish or crazy.

When I got married at the tender age of 23, I had no clue yet who I was. I was still insecure about myself and how I looked and unsure about what my beliefs were. Marrying someone much older, I thought I needed someone to tell me what to do, what to wear, how to cook, and when to clean. In short, instead of marrying purely for love, I wanted someone to tell me who I was. It was a time in my life when I based entirely too much of my self-worth on what other people thought of me.

It was crazy. I turned thirty and, wham, there I was. I'd *found* myself. Independent. Strong. Successful. Beautiful inside and out. It took years, but I'd come to realize, just like anything else in life, that people's opinions are subjective. And the only person's opinions that really mattered were my own. That revelation changed my entire being. It was the most freeing feeling in the world, yet also the scariest because it meant that my path was no longer the one I'd been following. It was time to follow my own road—one that only I would choose.

Where did that leave me and my family? Where did that leave my marriage? Mostly, where did that leave *me*? It took a long time, but I answered each of these questions; and I answered them solely on my own and from my heart.

While I believe that marriage requires compromise, I don't believe in compromise to the point where you sacrifice your own happiness. So I, the-glass-is-half-full girl, realized that my marriage was irreparably broken; and my husband and I divorced. To some, a marriage ending in divorce is a failure, but my marriage was also a success. I have two perfect, beautiful young children. I had eight years with a person who was, in all honesty, good to me overall. We built a family that may not have lasted, but one that I can be proud of now.

My ex-husband and I are coparenting. It's not always easy, but we have our children's best interests at heart. My family didn't break—it just became more unique. We are growing and creating two healthy hybrid families rather than one unhealthy and unstable one.

Where did all this leave me? It left me happy. Finally, truly, honestly happy. Not just with myself, but with the strength and courage it took to do what I knew in my heart was the right decision.

Stay together for the kids? Don't stay together and be miserable to show your children that they should *settle* and be miserable, too. An unhappy family together is not in any way better than a happy family apart. I'm a firm believer that no one should get married until they're 30 years old. Yes, I understand that there are a lot of you high school sweethearts out there who made it, like any other rule exceptions. However, the statistics prove that the number of divorces is on the rise. I believe part of the reason for this is marrying too soon. In our twenties we are still developing into the person we have yet to become. We are still designing ourselves, still a project in the making.

DARE TO PAIR

Sometimes the positive choices we make for ourselves result in rocky transitions and difficult fallouts. Rather than be angry about the things you can't change, embrace your own strength and look to a better future by sipping this minty, ripe-cherry flavored **Mad Housewife Cabernet Sauvignon**. Its explosion of sweet preserves and smooth, lush sensation of silky, mocha-like flavor will help make even the worst of times not seem quite as maddening.

My Fast Food Philosophy Flew the Coop

Before I had children, I would look at moms feeding their kids french fries and processed chicken nuggets and pompously nudge my friends, overtly judging those horrible moms for putting fast-food poison into their pure and developing babes. "I can promise you this: I will not take my child to a fast-food restaurant. I just don't want them growing up eating that type of food!"

Then I got pregnant. I stayed clear of caffeine, sushi, and soft cheeses. Of course, alcohol was nonexistent (except for a wine cooler on my birthday in my third trimester). I exercised through the first half of my pregnancy but, admittedly, also indulged in late-night root beer floats with my husband regularly. I drank tons of water, made sure I was eating plenty of greens to help my unborn baby thrive, and never missed my prenatal vitamin.

When my son was born, I proudly breast-fed. Working full time, I pumped religiously in a small bathroom in the office building where I worked. When it came time to start baby foods, I let myself down a little when I decided against utilizing the organic baby food cookbook I was given at my shower. However, I got over it and found myself challenged to search through the array of tiny jars on the grocery shelves for a balanced diet of veggies, fruits, and whole grains.

When my son was only six-months-old, I found out I was pregnant again, so I stopped breast-feeding and switched him to formula. As the months went by, I was excited about the pending birth of our second child and continued to take care of myself, occasionally giving into a bit of fast-food to ease my hectic lifestyle. Somehow I convinced myself that a chicken biscuit for breakfast was way healthier than a sausage biscuit.

When we welcomed the newest member of our family, breast-feeding again became my priority. Two days out of the week, we were lucky because my husband was home all day with the boys. The first time I called home to check on them, my husband proudly announced that our fifteen-month-old had just enjoyed his first hot dog ("dog-dog" as my son would soon call it). I was horrified.

First of all, hot dogs are the worst thing to give a toddler when it comes to choking hazards. Second, that was *so* not on our list of healthy foods! I kept it cool though and reminded him that the bites should be cut up in the tiniest of slices, always long ways, if he should desire to serve that to our child again. *Sweetly.* Not too long after that, I'd returned home from work to a recap of the day that included a road trip through the Wendy's drive-thru.

"He loves french fries!" My husband joyously announced.

My dream! My dream that my children would never experience fast-food evil had crashed right before my eyes.

Fast forward to a life with two toddlers. I'm now a stay-at-home mom, and I engage my boys in endless playdates, most are usually twenty minutes away from our house. Many scenarios find me racing home while trying to keep them awake in the car before nap time. The perfect solution: waffle fries and chicken nuggets. It keeps them awake the whole ride home and the extra bonus: no food preparation once we get there.

After an afternoon at the aquarium when their dad is working late, the beauty of the thought of no dishes to clean up after dinner wins, and I pull into a drive-thru. I swear I can get my kids to eat more while strapped in their car seats than I can at the table at home. To ease my guilt a little, I've learned that many fast-food restaurants offer apple slices so I've been able to swap them out for the fries *some* of the time.

DARE TO PAIR

While the kids drown their chicken nuggets in honey mustard, and you ponder where your ideals went, look forward to the sweet notes of honeysuckle in the **Paraduxx V Blend Napa Valley White Wine**. Relaxing with the creamy textures of apricot and white peach in this white wine will help you recall the fruit-and-yogurt dip you gave the kids, which means the day wasn't a complete flop. When your parenting philosophies fly the coop, sometimes you've just got to go with it.

On Facebook Again, I Feel Horrible for "Ignoring" My Children, But I'm Only Human

Every mother I've ever known has had it. *Mommy Guilt* they call it. It's a real, actual thing; regardless of whether you work or stay at home, volunteer at the school, go to every ballet practice or soccer game, you still have *it*. I've never met a mother who doesn't feel guilty about something. There is some comfort for me in knowing that I'm not the only one, but over time, I find that because there are way too many things to feel guilty about, I devote entirely too much time to *it*.

So what do we mothers feel guilty about? *Plenty.* Here are some examples of what made me feel guilty just in the last week.

For starters, I got annoyed because I had to ask Kate to do something for the fourth time with no response from her. So, I did what any other patient and loving mother would do: I raised my voice to her. Okay, I barked at her. *Yelled.* Nothing *mean,* but I did yell and it scared her because normally we laugh and joke and I can get a response without having to experience that kind of childish behavior (coming from me, mind you, not her). So there it was, the infamous #LostTemperGuilt.

Twice last week I allowed my children to have canned, sodium-filled chicken noodle soup for dinner because a) they like it, and b) most importantly, it's easy. Since I'm not exactly steering them toward sound nutrition in such *fine* moments, and when you consider the McDonald's I had let them have last week as well, #ContributingtoAmerica'sObesityProblem Guilt crept up on me.

One night this week, I put my kids to bed as I usually do—together in the same room. While they each have their own bedroom, they have been doing this for a couple of years now; and I think it's sweet and cozy for them. However, now that Kate is getting older she wants to sleep by herself, which I know will devastate her very dependent sister. At any rate, it was the end of the day, and my tank was beyond empty. They were arguing over how light their night-light should be. I told them they needed to "compromise" and work it out on their own. Of course, neither of them knows what this means, and I didn't bother to explain it to them. Instead, I got madder and madder at Meg's unreasonable (yet totally normal) fear of the dark and Kate's inflexibility. I told them just to work it out as I shut the door. #Laissez-FaireParentingGuilt. After an hour, they were still cracking and uncracking the door, neither of them was even close to sleep. Well played, Mama. *Well played.*

Back when I worked and was an important cog in the wheel of something other than American Girl trivia, I used to be on the computer all day, frequently accessing the Internet. That habit is hard to break so I still check e-mail, among other things. I need to be informed, right? So I look at the head-lines—have they released that poor hostage in Alabama? What is up with this crazy weather? What did one of the housewives from Washington, DC, do? The problem is I'm on the Internet instead of spending time with my precious children, the ones for whom I quit my job in order to be a "present" mother to.

Then there's Facebook, which must, of course, be checked regularly. What's everyone up to? I guess I do have a certain addiction to it. I didn't realize my Facebook use was as fre-quent as it apparently is until I read a recent school journal entry from Kate. The writing assignment was to describe what Santa does when he's not busy Santa-ing. Kate wrote a detailed essay about how he interacts with his elves, eats din-ner with Mrs. Claus, and checks his Facebook page. The only reason she knows what Facebook is is because Mama spends an exorbitant amount of time on it. This is a phenomenon known as #IgnoringYourChildreninFavorofAbsoluteDrivelGuilt, aka #FacebookGuilt.

Further, for another assignment she was told to name some characteristics of her mother. Among her responses: "lazzy" and "takes naps." Now, to be fair, Kate doesn't know that *lazy* carries with it a rather negative connotation, but she couldn't even spell it right, Perhaps if her mother would quit napping, she could help her spell words like *lazy*. (She did say I was "nice" so there's that—which was obviously before I yelled at her.) #NappingTooFrequentlyGuilt.

I've been getting e-mails all week about the girls' Valentine's Day parties at school. I've done nothing to contribute to them. Even though one of the reasons I stayed home from work was to be an involved parent, I have no idea what's being planned, what's been done, and what I need to do. Part of the issue is that I've gotten so many e-mails about all of it that I can't keep them all straight. How did I ever manage 450+ employees when I worked? At the office, I used to easily get more than a hundred e-mails daily; now the six a day I get totally confound me. In fairness to me, I've been unable to shake a stupid cold and have had no energy at all. I must say, though, I'm a little concerned that I am using this cold as a convenient excuse to be lazy (see above). #TrueColorsGuilt.

Right now, I'm self-conscious about the bags and dark circles under my eyes. I know my husband has noticed. I'm turning 40 this year so I feel as though it's all anyone can see when they look at me. #IApologizeforActuallyAgingGuilt.

Of course, then there is the favorite #IAmSuchaBitchGuilt. This one comes out whenever I am really frustrated and annoyed with my husband Mike and then he does something very sweet for me. And when it's my kids who frustrate me to the end of all reason, I take a step back and realize that one day all of that noise and mess in the room will be gone. #NotThankfulEnoughforWhatIHaveGuilt.

Sadly, I do not have the cure for all of this guilt. Part of getting better is admitting you have a problem, right? So maybe how you overcome guilt is to recognize it when it rears its ugly head and know what you'd be missing if you didn't have what triggers it.

So all of you moms and women out there, relax. Ease up on yourself despite #YourBestWillNeverBeGoodEnoughGuilt. Enjoy what you have when you have it. Most of us have more than we ever dreamed.

DARE TO PAIR

Stop badgering yourself and know that you're doing the best you possibly can. When the need arises, sip on the full-bodied **Nagging Doubt Chardonnay**, which boasts a wonderful citrus nose from the grapefruit the vineyard produces, along with brioche, pineapple, stone fruit, and green apple notes. Chardonnay is a nice basic wine for a mother's most basic feeling: Guilt.

Being My Children's Playmate 24/7

My two boys, five and almost four, are best buddies. Despite a house full of toys, they still need me or Daddy to play with them *all* the time—even after my five-year-old's birthday party. They can play on their own for a maybe 10 or 15 minutes and then it's: "I need someone to build a building with me" or "I want someone to draw with me," and my little doctor's favorite, "Who is sick and needs to go to the emergency room?" This game is also my favorite because it's just a matter of my husband or me "relaxing" on the couch—I mean, operating table. No matter the game or the toy, they want our participation. While I have a feeling that I must have been the same way as a kid, I wonder if my parents handled the parent-as-playmate demands differently than me.

I'm constantly saying, "Give me five more minutes" or "In just a second" or the popular "Go see if your brother will do that with you." He does ask him, but then his brother doesn't want to play the game followed by whining and tattling, *"He doesn't want to plaaaaayyyyy with me."* OMG! But, I *do* work from home and I am lucky to fit in playtime in increments all day. Seriously, I play with them *a lot*, each and every single day.

Still, I feel so guilty when I have to put them off. Yet I also feel resentful over how much they want me to play with them, then guilty over that. Then when I do play with them, I feel guilty because other things are sliding; and I wonder if I shouldn't be teaching them to manage on their own. I honestly can't decide if they should be playing more independently or if I'm letting these amazingly precious extra moments of Mommy-and-me playtime pass us by. Shouldn't I be seizing the moment?

I bought my five-year-old the boy equivalent of a doll house—a wooden fire station that opens up to 12 rooms including furniture. In my opinion, it's the most awesome boy's toy ever! The night he opened it, he played with it for a good hour. I was excited! I could see a future of him zooming his fire trucks around as he made the fireman slide down the pole. Independent play at its finest. The reality was that he quickly called out for someone to play the part of the other fireman. So there I was down on my knees teaching him how to make the firemen interact with one another, reliving my Barbie and Ken days.

DARE TO PAIR

After a long day's fight between filling their play needs and encouraging their independence, carve out some time for you and enjoy the **Playtime Red Wine**. It's a blend of Zinfandel with small amounts of Grenache, Petite, and Barbera, sprightly noted with blackberry, plum, spices, and a touch of vanilla. Hey, mommy needs to play too.

Maybe it's perfectly fine the way it is or maybe I need to do more to encourage them to play on their own. Either way, I need to let go of the guilt. Whether I ever find that miraculous balance between parent-playmate time and play-alone time, I reassure myself daily that my boys won't be small for long, and I just need to enjoy each and every second while it lasts.

I'm Too Hard on Myself Sometimes

My son can't go to preschool because it costs the same as half of our mortgage per month. To afford it, I'd have to get a job. It's the "which comes first" scenario, the chicken or the egg. I can't find a decent job unless I have the time to put into a search, but I won't have that time unless my son is in preschool. Enter mommy guilt.

My five-year-old is in kindergarten, away from home seven hours a day, five days a week. On the other hand, my four-year-old is stuck at home missing the best friend whom he spent 12 hours a day all summer playing with. I am now his only playmate. All of his other friends are in preschool or elementary too. He's lonely and my heart is sad for him—and for *me.*

I torment myself by telling myself that I could have prevented this. If I'd been saving money these last five years, he would be in a classroom right now using building blocks with Billy or laughing at something Julianna said. But, no, he's in the other room watching *Bubble Guppies*—alone—because I told him I needed twenty minutes to write.

Once again, I feel guilty. Once again, I catch myself in the "what ifs" and "if onlys."

I need to get my thinking on the right track. How? How can I set my priorities straight when I've made so many mistakes? I start to ask myself: are they truly mistakes? I mean, do all moms save money from the moment their kids are born for preschool? Probably not, but I still *feel* bad. I still feel that I could do better for my children. Then I read the following from Joyce Meyer Ministries:

"Someone needs to hear this today. As long as we know that God loves us and God is good then how can we ever doubt that he won't take care of our situations? We serve a God who sees and hears and he loves you and, whether you feel like it or not, if you've prayed and you are trusting him, he is on your problem. God is *working* on *your* problem. What you need to do in the meantime is stay calm, stay sweet, stay out of fear and keep on keepin' on."

Taking a deep breath, I realize that things really aren't that bad, that, like every other mom, I'm entirely too hard on myself. I will keep looking at the want ads while I also make time to play LEGOs with my son. The right job will come at the right time; and, anyway, he's going to spend plenty of time in school, at least the next 13 years! So while he's home with me now, I'm going to stop beating myself up about the things I can't change, the things I can't control. I'm going to just live *guilt-free*.

DARE TO PAIR

Be optimistic. Be *good* to yourself. Keep things light with a glass of **Be. Bright Pinot Grigio**. The defined floral notes and bits of citrus add vibrancy to this nice, light golden wine. It's crisp and fresh on the palate as the pear dominates with hints of peach–an instant taste of optimism.

I *Am* a Good Mother!

Does it make me a bad mom because I wish it were bedtime already? Or at least time to cook dinner so I can pour that glass of wine, hoping my husband will keep the kids entertained long enough for me to unwind, at least a little. Maybe this weekend I can get out for a bit. I haven't had a girls' night in forever—no one tugging on my pant leg, no "Mommy this" or "Mommy that," just a few drinks, appetizers, and some adult conversation.

As much as we all want to be perfect and strive to be good mothers, we often feel as though we're failing. A *good* mom wouldn't count the minutes until nap time, begging for a break from her children. A *good* mom wouldn't dream of a getaway with her friends, desperate for some alone time *away* from her family. But the truth is that this is exactly what good mothers think. *Good* moms deserve a break.

Here's the problem: we don't know that we're good mothers. We don't even have a definition for what a good mother is. Good moms *do* have breakdowns and snap at their kids. We do crave a night off, if not to enjoy a bottle of wine with girlfriends, then, at least, to have ice cream and watch a chick flick. Some days we give in to the nagging and let our kids watch cartoons for more than the appropriate amount of time just so we can get stuff done. We give our kids junk food as bribery and let them play Angry Birds one too many times. We dream about when our diaper and bottle days will be over because, in some far-off land, we know freedom awaits—even though we know, when those days come, we'll miss *this*.

Feeling guilty because nap time is the highlight of your day? Or because, rather than dreading rushing off to that 8:00 a.m. meeting, you are jumping for joy? Feeling bad for lingering at the office beyond five o'clock to finish last-minute tasks instead of rushing home to your babies? You're not alone. And, you're not a bad mom!

All this guilt actually means that you are a good mom, because it shows you *care*. The ones that don't care, for example, won't feel guilty when they don't take their kids to the park. They aren't concerned if their kids eat corndogs or McDonald's seven days a week. They don't need a break because they aren't involved or interacting enough with their children in the first place. They aren't asking themselves whether they are good or bad because they simply don't bother to even think about it.

You, on the other hand, *do* care. So smile, relax and enjoy nap time or the quiet of your train-ride commute. Have that glass of wine, now and then, guilt-free. Let go! Get dressed up and go out with your girlfriends and admit your faults. Talk about your parenting imperfections and laugh over your mistakes. Only by sharing stories and encouraging one another, will we all begin to understand what it truly means to be a good mother, which we already *are*.

DARE TO PAIR

In all the ways you really do care, you are the emblem of a good mother. Let the subtle undertones of chocolate, toffee, and toasted vanilla in the **Emblem Cabernet Sauvignon** remind you of all the under-the-radar things you do right, all the actions we as mothers don't give ourselves credit for. When it's time to reflect on your wins, we recommend the beautifully balanced, lush ripe fruit flavors that make up this delight.

CHAPTER 2

Frustrated

So much of a mother's life entails balancing the needs of her family with her own. Inevitably, mom's needs most often lose out. Having to set aside our own agendas and desires means resentment starts to build, compounded by normal daily frustrations as we try to juggle work, family, and life. As wonderful as being a mom can be, some days it definitely feels as though we traded in our freedom for motherhood.

When you're just about to fall off that tightrope you've been struggling to do a balancing act on, reach for one of the wines suggested in this chapter. A few slow sips and frustration will surely begin to melt away.

It's Nearly Impossible to Work from Home with the Kids Around

The words flow from my fingertips spelling out a story onto my computer screen: "It was a dark and stormy night. The wind made the branches from my Magnolia tree screech against the windows in my sun room . . ."

My head was in it. I was there in my novel, hearing the

creepy sound of the branches, smelling the hard rain through the screen door. I kept typing, "Out of the corner of my eye I saw a shadow dance. It made my heart skip a beat. It wasn't a shadow at all, it was . . ."

"Mom! Can have a snack? Mom! Mom!"

Ugh! My head dropped to the desk. Once again I am awakened from deep thought. It has been exactly one week since summer recess, and so far it is looking pretty good that I'm not going to get *any* work done this summer. I can't finish a single thought. It's only 9:45 a.m., and they 're asking for their 3rd "snack" of the morning. Apparently breakfast at 7:45 a.m. wasn't enough or the grapes at 8:30 a.m. or the health bar they split—what 15 minutes ago? I have to stop these snack attacks *now* or I won't survive the summer!

"No more snacks. You have to wait until lunch now. Go play with your brother." I guide my son by the shoulders as we walk step by step into the living room. "See all these LEGOs? Build an airport!"

Their eyes light up. "Great idea, mom," my oldest boy praises. And they go right to it.

Back in my office, where was I? I reread my last paragraph, close my eyes and put myself back into my story. That's right, it's her ex-husband who has shown up in the dark night. But, she doesn't know this yet. Ahhh, here we go: "'Michael?' His strong arm reached out to her as she gasped."

Ding. Dong.

Ding. Dong! Ding. Dong!! Ding. Dong!!! Di-iiiing. Dooooooooong!!!!

Good Lord! Rising quickly from my chair, I know very well there is no special guest at my door. It's my children who love to incessantly ring the doorbell, which not only drives me crazy but also starts my dog howling at each piercing tone.

I swing open the front door. "What are you doing? Get inside! I told you that doorbell makes Max nervous! Come inside."

I take a look at both of my boys. Maybe I need to get them outside for some fresh air, especially since it's not crazy hot yet. "Do y'all want to go to the playground?"

"Woooo hooo!!!" they scream. I don't think I've ever seen them race so fast to put their sandals on. "Let's go!" my youngest shouts out.

While we're at the park they have fun with some new play-mates while I sit with paper and pen under the shade of a Crape Myrtle. I may not have my laptop, but I can brainstorm and jot down some notes. My mind races once again and I find myself miles away, though I can still hear the pleasant laughter of my boys' voices in the near distance. Just as I'm jotting down a fabulous idea that came to mind, I am inter-rupted as my son cries out over skinning his knee. I rush to him. "It's okay! You're going to be fine. It's barely even bleeding." And with a sigh, "Come sit with me and have some of your lunch." The idea is *gone.* In between small conversation with the boys and unwrapping and peeling and slicing, I try to recover it. But, it's gone. I can only hope that—if it was such a great idea—it will come back to me.

A couple of hours later we're back at home. The boys are content in front of *Jake and the Neverland Pirates* so I'm once again alone with my computer. It just takes a minute of quiet to summon that lost idea back to me, and I finish the chapter. Since I have about an hour before we need to leave for the read-aloud time at the library, I decide to review the chapter. But, I don't get as far as the third paragraph before my child is standing at my door, "I'm hungry." Here we go *again.* The rest of the day is lost.

There's a silver lining: bedtime. Tucking them into bed for the night, I feel a surge of excitement knowing that I finally have a few hours to make some progress with the book. Soon I am back in my new cushy office chair, glass of wine within reach. As I began to read I find the flow that was missing all day due to so many interruptions. I'm able to think of new concepts, expand on ideas and even come up with some new ones. Ahhh, the *flow*. I read, critique myself, rewrite and feel powerful. I am accomplishing, fully engrossed in my work, no interruptions, no . . .

There's a knock at the door.

"Did I mention you look beautiful today," my husband peeks in with a mischievous smile. I can't feel annoyed this time. Closing my laptop, I give him a sexy look back. Maybe I'll do some research for when my heroine reunites with her ex. . . .

As for the work—there's *always* tomorrow.

DARE TO PAIR

While some work days only result in tortoise-like progress instead of hare-like strides, at least there's **Prosperity Red**. Very dark garnet in color, this simple Malbec seethes with the flavor of plums and other fruit with hints of yummy spice. It will melt even the most frustrating of days away with its robust yet mellow flavor.

Right Now, I Hate My Children

I wish my baby Sophia was five already so I could actually talk with the other moms. Every time we meet up, they all seem to be able to enjoy some freedom because their kids are old enough to play together. Even though Noah runs and plays, I'm still tied down with *this* one. My attention has to be on her as I hand her a cracker, bounce her on my knee, give her a toy, change her diaper, and/or give her a bottle. Damn! Can't a woman *breathe*?

At home, it's even worse because Noah gets bored so it's Mommy this and Mommy that. He won't play on his own. He'll *barely* stay still for an entire 24-minute episode of *Sponge-Bob*. And the boy is *always* hungry. Or maybe bored. And, he's always uses that whiney voice while breaking down each word into exaggerated syllables every time he wants something, "Let's goooo to the paaaark."

While Sophia is napping, and Noah is building a skyscraper out of big blocks, I use the first thirty minutes of this quiet time to finish the dishes and sweep the floor. Then I gleefully tip-toe to the couch to relax with my *People* magazine.

Crash!

"Dumb!" my son shouts. Checking out the situation, I find him kicking what's left of the plastic building that is crumbled on the floor.

Just then, I hear Sophia wailing from her room. There goes her two-hour nap. She never goes down again once she's-woken up. Now I'll have a cranky baby while I'm trying to cook dinner to boot.

I *hate* my life.

Just as I'm about to go in to check on her, my four-year-old is pulling on my shorts, "Mom! Help! Now! I need help." I'm always torn in two (or more) directions. Neither direction ever leads back to *me.*

On a good day, I love that Sophia is 13-months-old. I love the sweetness in her chubby little face. I love her wobbly walk. I love the sounds she makes and the way her eyes light up when she smiles. On a good day, I don't want Noah to ever be big enough to start kindergarten. I want him home for snuggles forever. On a good day, I *cherish* the moments with them.

Today is simply not one of those days. As I get down on my knees beside Noah, I can't help but think this is all too much. And that's when it occurs to me. It's not my *kids* that I hate. It's not my life that I hate. I hate feeling like I need help or a break. I hate feeling like I can't handle all of it with ease and patience and peace of mind. I hate feeling *this* feeling: frustrated.

I just wish I had a little more freedom or some more breaks now and then so I could appreciate the moments that *are* amazing and the patience for the ones that aren't. Then I'd deal better with *this* feeling.

DARE TO PAIR

Oy vey! At this point, it may seem like the only thing that can make you smile is something decadent and rich. Thank goodness for **Layer Cake Malbec** with its layer upon layer of savory fruit, spice notes, espresso, and dark chocolate for the palate as well as a rich, creamy texture and aromas of Asian spices, lavender, blueberry pie, and black cherry. It's making you feel better already, *isn't it*?

Can My Child Embarrass Me More?
Public Tantrums Are the Worst

I knew it was crazy having two boys within 14 and a half months of each other, but it's not like we planned it that way. (Some people swear by it, though, saying it's easier when they are close in age because they play together.)

As I stand outside of our apartment building after a rockin' afternoon at the playground, I'm faced with what appears to be the most humiliating moment of my life as a mom (to date).

Holding my seven-month-old in my arms, I watch as my nearly two-year-old throws his body to the ground, kicking and screaming, seriously unhappy about having to go home. I take a breath and look up the three flights of stairs I have to conquer in order to get us all inside and then glance around at the dozens of windows facing our show.

Someone is watching me. Someone is waiting to see how I handle this. Even if it's just God, this is a test in composure. I want to cry. I want to panic. But I know I have to act and teach my child a lesson. This is his first real tantrum, I mean, *full-body tantrum*. And since he's the oldest, it's my first tantrum too. Scenarios run through my head. I could try my sweet approach by kneeling down to his level and telling him not to worry, that we'll go to the park tomorrow. Obviously, my toddler will look up at me and say, "Oh, we can go again tomorrow? Fabulous! I didn't realize that! You're the best mom ever!"

Or I could take the stern route and tell him if he doesn't quit and walk up the stairs with me now, he'll go to bed early or lose his favorite toy for a day. But he's only almost two; he won't understand what that means. Ugh! I could really get tough and spank him to show him who's boss. But it's my policy not to spank—especially in today's world—in front of crazy neighbors. It's at that moment I realize my only option is to muster my supermom strength and carry both boys up all 31 steps—yes, I've counted! Whose idea, was it anyway to move to the top floor? Oh right, it was mine because I felt way safer up there. Well, hey, my calves are looking pretty shapely nowadays as a result!

So I sweep the kicking toddler up in one arm and lug both boys up the stairs and into the apartment in one piece. If he's not even two yet, I wonder, what will the terrible twos (times two) have in store for me?

Better not go there!

> ## DARE TO PAIR
>
> When your offspring mutates into a wild barbarian, you might want to take a swig of **Noble Savage Sauvignon Blanc**. From South Africa's Bartinney Private Cellars, it is less complex than your little one in the midst of a tantrum, this wine flaunts effervescent notes of grapefruit and granadilla for the nose, with refreshing green apple and citrus flavors for the palate.

I Woke My Preschooler from His Nap Far Too Early

It was Bizarro World at my house for about 30 minutes last night.

My three-year-old, Sawyer, who started napping again once he went into preschool, was home with me yesterday. We had a fun morning playdate at a friend's house, but we didn't get a nap in. Honestly, I didn't want him to nap because lately at bedtime just when his brother Owen is ready to sleep, Sawyer is ready to party if he's had that afternoon nap.

After preschool though, my sweet little angel fell asleep in the car on the way home and woke up just long enough to walk to the couch and pass out again. We'd made plans to go out to dinner, which I was really looking forward to, so I decided a catnap would be fine. Thirty minutes later, Daddy arrived home from work, all ready to go to dinner so I motioned to Jake that it was okay to wake his little brother.

Holy terror, Batman!

Appearing before us seemed to be a little boy who had been overcome by demons. I didn't know *who* this child was. For your information, Sawyer has probably thrown three good fits in his lifetime *tops*! He's always been our happy-go-lucky, go-with-the-flow little fellow. So meltdowns from him are so rare that the sobbing and moaning we were hearing left us speechless. He climbed up on my lap and burrowed his head into my neck, bawling. "I just want to sleep!" he cried.

I thought that if I held him for a few minutes, he'd calm down, then wake up some more and be ready to go. Typically it just takes a few a minutes and maybe a Yoo-hoo to break him from any post-nap delirium. Not this time. He only cried harder and louder.

My husband and I looked at one another, thinking the same thing: who is this person?

Coaxing him gently, my husband said, "Hey little buddy, you're just sleepy! Do you want to go get some french fries somewhere?"

French fries? He loves french fries! Surely, this would work.

"Noooooo!!!!!!!!!" tears gushed from his eyes and he burrowed himself back into me.

At that point, it had been 10 minutes and this was so unlike him, I was starting to assume he was coming down with a cold. I whisked him away to his dark room to lay him down and talk softly to him.

"Sweetie, do you feel okay?" I felt his forehead and he didn't feel warm at all.

"I just want to stay home!" he sobbed.

"Okay, we can stay. You can just rest and we'll eat here." I cooed. He nodded his head, calming slightly but still crying and clutching his blankie. I felt disappointment creep into my being. I wanted to cry. *Stay home?* I *always* stay home.

I ran downstairs and suggested to my husband that he and Jake go on without us and have a special "dad-and-son's night out." He was receptive, but he sensed my disappointment. Honestly though, I felt less disappointment about not going out to dinner than I felt dismay over my son's behavior. "I think he must be coming down with something," I said.

My husband decided he was going to try to talk to our youngster one more time. *As if he could do any better, I thought.*

Five minutes later, the two appeared downstairs, my son with a bright big smile on his face and wiping his eyes dry. He ran to me exclaiming, "Mommy, I feel better and we are all going to go eat dinner and I'm happy now!" Kneeling, I hugged him tight, kissed his cheek, and looked suspiciously up at my husband. *How? How? What kind of magic spells does this man know that can turn things around like this?*

My husband just smiled and said, "Daddy knows best. Just never let them see you sweat!"

Twenty minutes later, the four of us were sitting in a softly lit restaurant, with two glasses of red wine set on our cozy table, the guilt for putting my lovely boy through what he wasn't ready for becoming a distant memory. It turned out to be one of our best dinners out. I may have ended nap time too early, but Daddy Dearest had saved the day!

DARE TO PAIR

If your normally docile child has suddenly decided to have a mother of a tantrum—right at the wrong moment—the rich red wine of **Jekyll and Hyde Shiraz Viognier** by Hugh Hamilton Wines is for you. A full-bodied, richly textured wine filled with raspberry, cherry, and chocolate aromas and flavors, it is guaranteed to lighten *your* mood.

My Kids Are Attached to Me 14 Hours a Day

My boys have left me a few minutes while they play with a truck or dunk a basketball. I see my "out" and sneak four feet away to the laptop that sits conveniently on our breakfast bar, allowing me quick access to type away as I can, even though it means standing. Most of the time when this happens, not even 60 seconds goes by before my youngest toddler is poking me. "Up, Mama!"

I give in and pick him up, thinking he'll be content with me just holding him on my hip the way I did when he was 10 months old. No. He wants to type, or rather, bang on the keyboard. Or press a button. Or reach for my diet root beer. So down he goes and runs off to chase his older brother. I try to refocus on the task at hand. Was I checking my bank statement or researching something on the Internet?

I feel a pinch on my butt. He's back. Of course. I can't ever get anything done! So I participate in a new trick that occupies him for a good two minutes. I lift my right leg up in a ballet-type pose and rest it on the arm of our toddlerized couch. This allows my left leg to act as a pole for my little boy to circle round and round, thoroughly entertained. All right! I finish an e-mail. Score!

His older brother sees this fun from across the room and joins in. Before it ends with the two of them knocking heads, I've managed to balance my budget. I'm excited I'm taking care of bizniss! This is the longest stretch of time I've had since last night when they went to bed. My two-and-a-half-year-old is now tugging at my pants, the drawstring coming loose and the waist band slipping way past my behind.

My son laughs. "I see your bootie!"

I corral them into the living room for some dancing. With Madonna and the Black Eyed Peas on the TV, we have fun, twirling and laughing. They soon get distracted and move on to their Jeep. I'm quick to take advantage and jump up to get some more work done.

As though my legs have some sort of magnetic force that neither of them can stay away from for too long, my oldest decides to use his latest technique to get my attention—ramming his whole body into my leg like I'm a tackling sled on a football field. (If this is the sport he ends up excelling in, I'll retract my annoyance with it). I steady myself holding the countertop with one hand, while I continue to use the mouse with my right. I'm in what has got to be some great yoga pose, before hearing him tell me he did something sweet for his brother, and therefore deserves candy as a treat. "No!" he shouts at me in the deepest voice he can muster when I refuse him the candy and stomps off.

Just as I'm about to finish typing my last sentence, my youngest little man is underneath me again, both arms wrapped around my knee, "Jooss," he says with adorable, needy eyes. I sigh and decide to call it a day, grabbing his juice and joining him and his brother in the living room for some snuggling and cartoons. There's no guarantee, but at nap time, I'll try again.

DARE TO PAIR

When it starts to seem as though they'll be attached to you forever, it's time to pour this deep and full-bodied Celani Family Vineyards **Tenacious Red Wine** boasting of tea and chocolate. The bouquet of plum blossoms, those first flowers blooming before the spring, will remind you that to all things there is a season—in other words, they won't be clingy forever!

I Made Time for *Me* Today

The door shuts behind me and a vast blue sky and fresh air welcomes me. Now it's just me—not mom, not wife, not daughter, or friend or Luke's mom. Just me. Nice to meet you world.

As I take in my first deep breath and begin to run to the rhythm of Robin Thicke's "Blurred Lines," my feet pound out a beat. I have barely been running five minutes when I already feel my shoulders relax. Even though tunes are radiating through my earbuds, quiet envelopes me. That's one thing about being a mom. Quiet can be surrounded by music—as long as it's not screaming or demanding children—it's still quiet to any mom. Oh, the peace! This is the one chance for me to be me—to be *free*.

The farther I run, the *more* alive I feel. The kids' busy schedules, the house we're trying to sell, and my frustrations suddenly seem less overwhelming. Everything is falling into perspective, and now it feels like I can handle it all. That's when I realize it—I'm actually smiling! The runners and families walking past me must think I'm crazy. But I don't care, I keep running.

By my second mile, I've convinced myself I *can* write that book that's been brewing in my mind and realize I *do* have the stamina to remodel the kitchen. As for that energy missing last night when my honey wanted a little action, why, I'm *full* of moxie now! The surge of vitality and confidence running through me encourages me to conquer the world. All this just from taking a short, three-mile run?

I spent the winter studying mindfulness. *This* is mindfulness. I'm aware of my whole body, my whole being. The sunshine sparkles on the bay as I run past a great blue heron fishing for his morning meal. God is all around me! I must do this more often, I think to myself.

My run is complete. After I stretch; I lie down on the floor. My two children see this as a fantastic opportunity to jump and climb on me, which I welcome with a smile and laughter. Running is imperative for me, not only for my health, but because it truly makes me a better mom.

You see it isn't the three-mile run that brings back my sanity and vitality, that eases my daily frustrations. It's the thirty minutes to myself, the fresh air, the time to think my own thoughts. It's the time to *breathe*. I run to *catch* my breath.

DARE TO PAIR

When opportunity arises for you to do something for yourself, be it a run or a warm bubble bath, you already know what it means. You're free to finally be *alone*. Explosively savory, the **Freedom Run Winery Estate Cabernet Franc** delivers a hint of the psychic freedom you desire along with notes of tobacco, bay leaf, and spice complimented with the fruit flavors of black cherry and blackberry. Who knew?

My Children's Silliness Gave Me Relief from My Stressful Day

I was driving home from work with both boys in the backseat. I was already in a funk after another long, stressful day at work, and they were being totally obnoxious.

A Red Hot Chili Peppers song was playing on the radio. I cranked it up in an effort to relieve some of my frustration and tune out the noise behind me. It didn't take long to realize that that particular song may not be appropriate for my kids.

I turned down the music, and a second later I hear my two-year-old Chase loudly announce: "SUCK MY KISS!" I look in the rearview to see him doing some serious eyebrow-crinkling, nose-wrinkling head bobbing, then once again scream, "SUCK MY KISS!"

I am grinning—it simply can't be avoided—because then my four-year-old Colton states, "Chase, that is not a song, this is a song: 'Old McDonald had a farm, eeh i eeh i oh.'"

My stress and frustration began to vanish, leaving my body, as my boys and I laughed out loud and rocked to the music. Thanks to those precious babies I no longer had a worry in the world.

DARE TO PAIR

Because our children are truly our greatest escape, revel in their beauty and ability to transform even our worst of days with a glass of this fruity **Big House The Great Escape Chardonnay**, containing hints of citrus and bold flavors of baked apple, vanilla, and subtle toasty oak.

CHAPTER 3

Overwhelmed

This chapter will no doubt have you thinking, "been there, done that" because we all battle the daily challenges and burdens of motherhood. Every new mother feels overwhelmed at first, but there are also days that will have even the most seasoned mom praying for an exit. Whether you're exhausted—which goes hand in hand with motherhood—or once again striving to be perfect (followed by an imminent #epic_fail), or feeling as if your days of breastfeeding may never end, we, ladies, have all *been there*.

When you feel as though all you need is a break, take a deep breath and look no further. This chapter has a plethora of wines that perfectly fit your ultimate need to simply *relax*.

Everyone Has Seen or Touched My Boobs by Now

I'm sure someone warned me that upon childbirth all modesty flies out the window. First of all, on the delivery table, they have you essentially naked in a small gown with legs spread-eagled for all to see. Then nurses arrive to look around in there, poking and prodding to supposedly diagnose progress. If I had known how many people would be staring at my hoo-haw, I may never have had the guts to give birth!

Immediately after the doctor pulled this huge being (okay, maybe not so huge, but it sure felt like it!) out of my body, I didn't even have a second to recoup before the nurses were grabbing my breasts, trying to find the perfect position for my baby boy to feed. We spent the next hour of his life letting him suck, let go, and then latch back on. It was apparent that hardly anything was coming out and my poor son was becoming frustrated, crying in between feedings.

The next few days in the hospital weren't much better. Every time a nurse came in, she plopped out one of my breasts, as if it's one of her medical tools, and pressed my son to me. She didn't hesitate to stick her hands in my gown to help readjust as needed. She kept reminding me that we have to get the position right or I'd be sorry later.

My milk still hadn't come in, but when it did it was enough to make someone want to lose it. My boobs inflated as big as balloons; my poor nipples were stretched beyond belief and leaking. I was so sore, I just wanted to have a hot bath and forget about this entire ruckus. My son had a different agenda.

By the time I left the hospital, I vowed if anyone ever touched my boobs again, I might punch their lights out. But, within an hour, I was sitting at home doing guess what? You got it: *breast-feeding!* I couldn't go anywhere because my precious angel had quite the appetite and was basically attached to me 24/7. Didn't somebody say this was supposed to be a time of bonding? If masquerading as an open-all-night diner equals "bonding," I guess that's what was happening.

Within a few days of being home, my breasts were still sore, and blisters surrounded my nipples. He had obviously been latching on wrong. That damn nurse was right! Off to the hospital I went for one more poor woman to grope my boobs and show me what I was doing wrong.

It's amazing what mothers can endure, it truly is. Eventually, my son and I got the breast-feeding thing down. We'd feed at pretty much the same times so I was free to do things in between. But, hey, when the time called for it, nobody said feeding in the car, pulled over on the side of the road, was a bad thing. Desperate times call for desperate measures.

At three months, when I had to return to work, I decided to let breast-feeding go and buy bottles and formula. Rather than be elated as I'd been expecting, I was depressed. I went back and forth on the decision probably a hundred times, driving both myself and my husband crazy. Deep down, I'd become attached to those moments together, rocking and feeding my son, and giving him something no one else could. Those first few months breast-feeding were tough, but then I didn't really want to let it go when I had to.

DARE TO PAIR

Motherhood comes with a lot of overwhelming changes to our bodies. Plus, soon after becoming a mom, we quickly realize that our bodies are no longer ours alone.

Every once in a while, take a page out of the old-you's notebook and perk up those (just slightly saggier) breasts with a nice, push-up bra and tight-fitting top and forget that everyone has touched them. Embrace *this* body image with a glass of the equally sultry **Marilyn Merlot**, with aromas of ripe cherry and strawberry. Even just the collectors-style label that graces the bottle will make you feel sexy and flamboyant again.

No One Told Me It Would Be *This* Challenging

I didn't plan on having children. I liked kids, but my husband and I were too wrapped up in our professional lives and our life with each other so we had decided to stay childless. Then one day—*surprise!*—we were pregnant, even after taking the appropriate measures to ensure it wouldn't happen. After a few meltdowns, it didn't take long for me to see the positive, and I immediately began to prepare for motherhood.

I'm very structured and don't like the *unknown*, preferring to know what to expect and when. To prepare for my little baby boy's arrival, I sucked in all the knowledge I could—even watching TV shows that pertained to parenthood.

When Kesel James was born, there was no way I could be prepared for that special little boy or the love I felt for him. We may not have wanted children, but this little angel filled my heart with joy and brought tears to my eyes. No one could have truly explained to me the emotions you feel toward your newborn baby.

As the weeks wore on after we came home, I realized again that nothing could've gotten me ready for the craziness that ensued. Sure, everyone tells you to expect to get zero sleep. They warn you to expect a crying baby who can't tell you what he needs and that you aren't going to be able to control every aspect of this particular situation, no matter how hard you try.

But nobody mentioned that it would take me more than an hour just to prepare for as mundane a task as simply going to the grocery store. Getting *just* the diaper bag and Kesel ready involved packing diapers, formula, and an extra outfit just in case—all this for just a trip to the store! No one warned me that the minute I'd finally be ready and begin to head out the door he'd poop or spit up all over himself, causing me to turn around and start the darned process all over again.

I also wasn't warned that one of the perils of motherhood

is car rides. It takes a while to get used to putting your baby *in* the car seat as well as getting him *used* to the car seat. For a new mother, a 15-minute ride to the store may take 45 minutes or more by the time you stop, find the pacifier, and soothe him. Is he hungry again? Honestly, I don't know how breast-feeding mamas do it!

Then you get to the store, and it's an entirely new battle zone. You're trying not to imagine all the germs around you as the person next to you in the produce aisle coughs or wheezes. You try not to stare at the dirty little boy with grimy hands touching everything in sight, infecting it all with any sort of bacteria he may have on him. The shopping process that used to take less than an hour is now twice as long because, again, you're soothing, feeding, changing diapers—whatever it takes to keep this little being from wailing and disrupting the entire store, as well as your sanity.

By the time you're finally home, especially after the first time, you swear you'll never do it again. Until the next time. No soon-to-be first-time mom can even begin imagine the craziness of being a new mother. All you can do is just brace yourself for a bumpy ride and take on the challenges as they come.

DARE TO PAIR

Frenzy Sauvignon Blanc is inspired by the myriad, uncontrollable forces of nature that must fall into place in order to make great wine. Thus, it is a perfect match for when we are contemplating the infinite, unpredictable moments of parenthood that challenge us to be great mothers. Hopefully, the harmony of the peach, grapefruit, lime, melon, and fresh-cut grass characteristics of this Sauvignon Blanc will lend a little harmony to your life after a hectic day.

A Magician, I'm *Not*

Though at times it may seem that I'm a mom with the bewitching talent of being able to make multiple things happen at once; I must finally confess to you, my *dear* family: I'm not a magician. I know, I know. *Shocking!* Please, sit back, and I'll make this easy on all of us.

This isn't about me *not* wanting to do all the things I do with and for you. I do. I really, *really* do! I just can't do them all at the exact same time immediately when you ask me to. Please realize that, if I could, I would make all your desires happen for you all at once, my precious doves. Well, maybe, within reason, of course. But, honestly, I just can't do it all at the same time. So here is your lesson for the day and maybe it will help you learn that patience is a virtue.

Here are just some examples of what I cannot accomplish all at the same time:

- *Really* hear what each of you is demanding as you summon me at three different decibel levels.

- Make you another waffle while pouring a glass of milk and helping your brother wipe his behind.

- Clean the kitchen while playing Mario Brothers with you and drawing with your brother.

- Pick the pepperoni from your pizza while taking the brown stuff off your brother's broccoli and refilling the dog's water bowl.

- Put the laundry in the dryer while reheating the chicken you didn't touch at lunch while peeling a Band-Aid from your lovely leg.

- Wipe the syrup from your apple slice while finding your lost shoe and taking the dog outside to go potty.

- Find the note you hid while picking up teeny, tiny pieces of Play-Doh and helping you jump fire in your new Mario game.

- Snuggle with both of my arms wrapped around you while handing you your water and helping your brother pull up his pajamas.

Ahh, to be *Bewitched*'s Samantha who simply twitched her nose to keep her household running smoothly. . . .

DARE TO PAIR

Tonight, you *can* be Samantha. Wiggle your nose over a glass of the somewhat dry **Bewitched Pinot Noir** by VML Wine. Smooth yet complex, this is a pleasing presentation of rich strawberry and cherry with a magnificent burst of vanilla bean. Notes of caramel and maraschino cherry top this majestic night-off swirl.

I Haven't Slept in a Week!

I am crying out loud right in sync with my one-year-old's desperate sobs. It's early March, and a round of colds found its way into our home, attacking my husband and two-year-old first before it took hold of my baby. Funny how I always dodge these things yet somehow still suffer their effects.

I'm exhausted! The kind of exhausted where you pass a mirror and don't recognize who's looking back at you. The kind of exhausted where your educated mind truly can't reason out the possibility that you will *ever* find sleep again. The kind of tired where your tears actually burn your eyes, begging you to *please* shut them tight.

My husband's snoring kept me up earlier in the week, followed by a couple of nights spent waking up every hour to care for my coughing and wheezing toddler. With him finally sleeping through the night again, I am now on night two with my baby boy, who seems to have gotten the worst of it.

So here I am—going on almost a week with just a few hours of sleep each night. How is it that I have the energy to rock my son, hold him tight through his tears, and comfort him when I feel like my body is about to shut down from sleep deprivation? Even so, I try everything, and nothing works.

An hour goes by, and finally his eyes close as he rapidly sucks in the last of his throbbing cries. I start to relax. My shoulders settle into the couch, my back following suit as I breathe a sigh, and my eyes roll back in my head. Then, like a black cat jumping out from behind a plant in a 1970s horror flick, he cries suddenly so that my whole being tenses again. But his eyes are still closed and his sobs taper off. His chest peacefully rises and falls to the rhythm of relief. I start to cry again, muffling every sound with a pillow. Looking at the clock, I know that, even if I could fall asleep at this point, I'd only get two hours in because after that it's time for my older son to wake up and for my husband to head out to work.

I wasn't going to make it! Isn't this how even the strongest of mothers break?

I drag myself up and over to the window. The moonlight shines a message of comfort to me. I can't be alone in this. There has got to be another mother out there going through the same exact thing. Another mother lying awake somewhere, wishing she could just get some sleep.

And then I realize that it's these moments that make us mothers. It's not just that first step, or the first smile, or even the first word. It's the first tooth and soothing your baby through that terrible pain. It's the first real cold and the helplessness you feel as you try to do everything you can to make them feel better. It's the endless string of sleepless nights you endure, all because you are a mother. It's the grit, the tears, and the heartache we feel because we love these little beings more than ourselves, except we're too delirious sometimes to always realize it. That's what makes us true mothers. It's these moments that make it possible for us to appreciate the wonderful times. Without them, none of the good would have been earned.

I look over at my son perfectly nestled on our couch and fall onto the opposite sofa finally letting sleep overtake me.

DARE TO PAIR

An afternoon nap for Mom can be the best medicine after sleepless nights. If the universe didn't send one your way today—hell, even if it *did*—a swirl of a glass of **Siesta Cabernet Sauvignon**, from Ernesto Catena Vineyards, unlocks hints of lavender, a scent that research has proven soothes and relaxes. Tonight, unwind with the complex mélange of licorice, vanilla, cocoa, and baking spice.

Being a Pre-Step Mom Simply *Ain't* Easy

You never imagine yourself divorced, let alone, in a new relationship introducing a new man to your children. Even if you are a child of divorced parents, you definitely don't imagine yourself navigating that same landmine—no matter how pessimistic you may be.

Yet here I am: a newly single, divorced young momma with two young children. Nice to meet you. Next, meet new boyfriend. Oh, let's complicate things further by introducing my ex-husband, the new boyfriend's crazy ex-girlfriend, and, of course, their daughter. It just got real, right?

When the boyfriend's daughter enters the picture, it means you have just taken the new, fun relationship to a serious status by introducing each other to your children.

No, we're not married yet, and I have no idea if we'll even ever get married. Actually, you can't even make that decision until both of you have spent time with each other's children. The problem is, by bringing the children into the equation, you've already complicated everything. Goodbye sexy new relationship, hello married life—even though you're not married. Holy hell, how'd I sign up for this?

Then, once you get beyond the "hellos" and "how are you's?" of meeting the kids, it all ratchets up. Let's chat about: discipline; sleeping arrangements; kissing in front of the children; staying the night; aka, sleepovers; Sharing; helping; co-parenting. . . . Screw it—I'm out.

Okay, not really, but I will say that becoming a stepparent before you're actually a stepparent is one of the most challenging things in the world. None of the books prepare you for it. It can also turn out to be quite a rewarding experience. I was lucky. My boyfriend's daughter adored and respected me almost immediately. She fell right in step with our family routine and fit in perfectly with my children.

This doesn't mean it didn't get complicated when she tried to crawl in bed with us the first or second time, but we figured it out. It doesn't mean I didn't wonder where my boundaries were—or how to identify hers, but we dealt with it. It didn't take long before we started to be accustomed to our new family life, whatever that might mean to someone else.

My children also adored my boyfriend. He could never take the place of their father, but rather offered a different type of fathering experience than their dad. It felt as if between both men, my kids had the best of both worlds. Call me optimistic, but it all was becoming clear to me: we may not be your modern-day Cleavers, but we'd adopted our own type of happy and normal.

The hardest part for me was and always has been introducing someone into my life who I knew may or may not stay. I'm an all or nothing kind of woman, so I immediately took my boyfriend's daughter in like she is my own child. But whenever we fought and I thought that it might all end, all I could think about was ripping him out of my children's lives and him taking her out of mine. With the wounds from our previous breakups so fresh, it would take a long time to heal from a trauma like that—for everyone.

DARE TO PAIR

Today, the blended family is common, but that doesn't mean it's easy to combine so many people, each with his or her own personality. To assist during those difficult, sometimes overwhelming times of figuring it out, treat yourself to Ransom Wine's **Jigsaw Pinot Noir**, containing a scent of red cherry and rose, accentuated by lush flavors of crushed raspberry and hibiscus. These flavors blend seamlessly together in the jigsaw, just as you and the pieces of your family puzzle will, too.

The truth is: nothing is known. My marriage didn't last, so my new relationship might not either. It's complicated and it's messy. But isn't that what we mothers *do?* We can only offer our hearts with love and try to follow our intuition. We may make mistakes, we may let people in that we shouldn't but, in the end, if we didn't try, we'll never know. And maybe, just maybe, even if this new relationship doesn't work out, we'll both have had a positive impact each other's children's lives—one we'd have forever been without had we not been together.

Today I Feel like a Bad Mom

Once again it's Monday and I feel lousy because I have a million things to do—work, laundry, cleaning, and even grocery shopping. With children, it takes at least an hour to shop for the week. At least. To top it off, shopping with my children is anything but calming to my raging hormones. Yep, that's right—I'm deep into PMS. Fabulous!

On the upside, today is a gorgeous, sunny day. Neighbors are stopping by, asking us to meet them at the pool. Friends are texting, inviting us to the beach. And, I promised my boys a trip to the library and the zoo this week. Unfortunately, none of this is happening today.

I can only find a window of five minutes to color with my oldest. I can only race "one more" race when my youngest son wants me to race three more. No, 17. No, "Six more races, mom! Pleeeeeease!" Even as I do, I'm anxious to get back to my long list of tasks for the day. Any other day, I can handle the balancing act, even any other busy Monday. Today however, my mind can't take it. I'm feeling frazzled. I can't breathe. I want to cry.

Plus, they're bored. It's summer vacation. One son is surrounded by toys, games, and his big brother, yet he's still tugging at me, desperate over how he has "nuhhhhh-thiiiiiing" to do. The other son is telling me he can't breathe simply because he doesn't want to eat his blueberries. Seconds later he changes his excuse to he's "too tired" and has to rest his knees before he can eat said blueberries. Then, there's tattling. And hitting. And screaming. It's boys being boys, but I want to join in on the screaming myself. But, I can't—*someone* has to be reasonable.

So understandably I'm irritable and snap at them one too many times, which, of course makes me feel terrible. I start to lose it. I attempt to pull it together after a quick cry in the bathroom. At this point, I'm begging Auntie Flow to arrive already just to relieve me of this craziness. Why can't I get a hold of my emotions, get control of my to-do list and balance business with pleasure?

Today, I'm officially a bad mother. Or at least, I definitely feel like one.

Between PMS, my crazy boys, and this insane day, I decide to take a break from it all and bring the boys outside for a while—no neighbors or friends, just a nice long walk. Fresh air never hurt anyone. I realize that, even though the day is quickly passing me by, and I'll never get everything on my to-do list done, at least I'll keep my sanity. The laundry and dishes will still be there when I get home, but this fresh air has turned out to be a necessity. As I watch the boys race down a hill to get a better glimpse of some ducks, I breathe. I suck in air and—finally—breathe.

On the way home I realize that when it comes to choosing between housework and kids, I should always choose the kids. There will always be dirty dishes, laundry and a long grocery list. So instead of stressing about what I'm not getting done, I will try to revel in my babies while they are young and each day as they grow. Today, I may feel like I can't cope, but, deep down, I know that I'm truly a great mom, doing the very best with what I've got.

DARE TO PAIR

Whether or not you figure it out on your own or you need to talk it out, **Therapy Sauvignon Blanc** is just what the doctor ordered for a conflicted, tough day. This white wine has unique, therapeutic aromas reminiscent of passion fruit, boxwood and herbs, while the palate contains flavors of sweet and simple citrus.

It Can All Be Mended

My family was devastated when we lost our home in a fire. People who have not experienced this kind of tragedy truly do not understand its aftermath. You lose everything. It's not just the furniture, toys, and clothing—it's all the pictures, trip mementos, photos, and so on that really break your heart. Then there is the chaos of living out of boxes while your house is being rebuilt. They say that moving is one of the top five stressors. With a seven-year-old rambunctious boy on top of it—we were at our wits end.

After 10 long months, the day came when the repairs to our home were finally finished. We were so excited to get everything moved in. I imagined a clean, fresh start because this was like a brand-new house. My excitement didn't last long however.

Within hours of the furniture being delivered, our precious son Carson vomited all over it. Then, he drew on our newly installed carpet with a bright red marker. The fun didn't stop there. He proceeded to sneak a milk upstairs (which was forbidden) and spill it on the new carpet. We found out after it had curdled, of course. As if my patience hadn't been tested enough, I walked into the kitchen only to discover a gigantic scratch down the middle of my brand-new, stainless-steel refrigerator.

Let's not forget our next adventure. I hired a sitter for a few hours while I went out. When I got home, I discovered a bird had gotten into our new garage. Upon further inspection, I found five BB gun holes in the walls from Carson trying to scare the bird out.

I sighed and threw my hands up in the air in exasperation at the time, but looking back now, I have to smile. Our brand-new (old) home that we'd worked tirelessly to rebuild became home again in just a few days thanks to the efforts of our loving, sweet little boy.

DARE TO PAIR

Because there's no solution to your kiddos adding to the character of your home, savor the delicate aroma and taste of this light and buttery **Rascal Pinot Noir**. With cherry overtones and a texture soft as cotton, you'll soon toast the permanent memories—from spilled milk to holes in the wall—that your little rascals create in your home.

CHAPTER 4

Worried and Afraid

*E*veryone feels the pressures of today's modern life, and because moms often make the majority of the day-to-day decisions on running the household and parenting, the pressure's on *us*. We can't help but worry that our choices are the right ones and that we even have it in us to do the job. Then there are the things that are truly scary: a child disappearing, unforeseen weather on a river float, or the health crisis of a child. Nobody promised us it would be easy.

These are the times we just need to let go, even if only to take the edge off. Enter *wine*. While we do not encourage drinking as a coping mechanism, we do embrace it as a commemoration of the good, the bad, and the ugly of motherhood—because you most definitely can't have one without the others.

What if I Can't Live Up to the Promises I Made My Children?

Mothers make a simple promise to their newborns: to love them and care for them, no matter what it takes. However, this promise means that it doesn't take long before some complicated fears take root in our minds. In other words, mothers *worry*.

With unexpected economic heartbreak, career detours, and the everyday challenges that life is sure to deliver—and does—some of the promises we make to our children may feel like illusions. I learned this myself when things shifted dramatically for my husband and me. Suddenly I had to penny-pinch and cut coupons. It wasn't like we were poor, but for the first time in a long time, I had to pay attention to my spending.

I soon realized that with our smaller income, new Gap and Gymboree outfits wouldn't be filling up my boys' closets. We wouldn't be living in an upscale neighborhood with huge homes and white-picket fences. I wouldn't be having gigantic, ridiculous birthday parties (which my kids likely wouldn't remember anyway because they were too young).

All moms have lofty dreams of what they can offer their children. We promised not only to be responsible but to offer them the best that life has to offer. But can we? Reality will usually cause these ideals to be brought down to earth. And when this happens, we become afraid that we will fail our children. The truth is that our implicit promises will always exceed what we can really do so it's important to keep in mind what really matters.

NEWBORN

MOTHER: I promise to give you all the love and care you will ever need, and more.

CHILD: Please promise to do exactly that.

AGE 2

MOTHER: I promise you'll have a big, grassy, fenced-in yard to play in.

CHILD: Please promise to spend quality time with me, whether it's inside our home or outside at the park.

AGE 3

MOTHER: I promise I'll give you a little sister or brother.

CHILD: Please promise to provide me opportunities to socialize with other kids my age and to not just sit me in front of the television all day.

AGE 5

MOTHER: I promise you I'll send you to the best schools.

CHILD: Please promise to spend one-on-one time with me after school, helping me with my homework and teaching me all that you know.

AGE 10

MOTHER: I promise I'll take you to Disney World.

CHILD: Please promise to really listen to me, support my interests and let me explore my independence.

AGE 13

MOTHER: I promise I'll buy you all the right clothes.

CHILD: Please promise to teach me to be confident in myself, no matter what I'm wearing.

AGE 16

MOTHER: I promise I'll buy you a car.

CHILD: Please promise to teach me how to save money and earn the things that I want to have.

AGE 18

MOTHER: I promise I'll send you to the college of your choice.

CHILD: Please promise to carve a path for me so I do well in school, want to go to college, and do what it takes to get there.

If we're providing our kids with the essentials of love and security, direction and guidance, they will survive. More than likely, if we are the type of mothers that even have these worries, our children will *thrive*. Isn't it true that what we're already providing them is all they really need? We can get so hung up on giving them all the bells and whistles—the best schools, mind-blowing vacations, and the trendiest clothes, but what really matters are the simple times you spend with them as you give to them of yourself.

DARE TO PAIR

By understanding that all moms have worries and fears, you'll be a little less hard on yourself as a mother. When you start to doubt yourself, at the end of the day, raise a glass of this the spicy, dark-berry, red currant, and mocha flavored wine, **Pride Cabernet Sauvignon**, in gratitude of all that you *do* have and provide for your children.

My Son Ran Away

I had plenty to do that day—that was for sure. With two young children, two large labs, and their daddy working out of town, my plate was completely full. "Finn, take your sister and go outside to play." I knew my chores would take me a fraction of the time if I could keep the kids occupied for a bit, playing in our large, fenced-in backyard. I watched as they ran outside and grabbed the vacuum.

Only about ten minutes went by when I thought I heard crying. I shut the vacuum off and peered out the window. My 2-year-old, Acey, was sobbing. I ran outside to see what was wrong. There sat my little girl on top of the Rubbermaid trash can.

"What's wrong Acey?" I asked as I ran over to her.

"Finn put me up here, and I can't get down." She replied, plain as day. That girl has no trouble talking—or expressing herself.

I pulled Acey off the trash can. "Where's Finn?" I asked her.

"He ran away. He went over the fence and ran that way, mom." She pointed down the road.

I felt a small sense of panic creep through me. Ran away? That wasn't like Finn. I grabbed Acey and rushed toward the minivan. "He said he was going to the park to play with a friend," she helpfully told me as I strapped her into her car seat.

Now, I'm relying on my two-year-old to find my missing four-year-old.

I knew what park she was talking about though—the park at the high school where I coach volleyball. Finn and Acey often went there with me. Backing out of the driveway to the dirt road by my house, I paused. Which way would he go? There's a highway on one side and another dirt road on the other—both could lead to Big Horn High School, where I was sure—and hopeful—I would find Finn. I took the back way and sped along the dirt road, scanning ahead of me to see if I could see my little boy anywhere.

The small amount of relief I'd felt when Acey had announced Finn's destination was quickly squashed when I neared the paved road. Surely he hadn't made it this far? And surely he hadn't gone the highway route?

I turned into the school's parking lot, trying to control my fears. Freaking out wasn't going to help anything right now. A stream of cars was coming to and from the parking lot, and I realized that it was the last day of school. People were everywhere! How would I find Finn now? I scanned the playground, No Finn. Oh God! What do I do now?

Driving the car back the way I had come, I headed back toward home. Do I call my husband? Do I call the police? What the hell do I do? Just as I was turning onto the next road and about to lose it completely, I saw Finn from a distance on the highway, riding towards home on Acey's Strider Bike. I gunned it back to the house; and we arrived at the same time.

I slammed the car door and rushed toward Finn yelling, "What the heck were you doing? Finn, why did you run away? Do you know how scared that made me?"

"I got bored because you wouldn't play with me, so I left." He replied. Then he continued on, telling me his ultimate four-year-old plan. Even I had to admit, it sounded like a great plan. While he had wanted Acey to come to the park, too, he hadn't been strong enough to lift her over the fence, so he had decided to go down to the park, get one of his friends, and bring him back to help lift his sister over the fence. I didn't know whether to laugh, reprimand him, or just stare at him in awe.

The motherly side won. "Finn, you can't just leave home on your own. There are bad people in this world. They could have taken you! Not to mention, you could have been hit by a car, and then I wouldn't be there to help you." (Of course these were all the terrible scenarios that I had run through my head while I was desperately searching for him.) "Does that make sense? Do you understand? Don't do that ever again!"

I hugged him tight; then hugged Acey tight too. I don't know if it was a higher power watching over and protecting my children that day, but I was thankful. My son may have scared the living daylights out of me, but he was okay. The vacuuming, the dog hair, the dishes could wait. We were all *okay.*

DARE TO PAIR

There's nothing as likely to drive you over the edge as your fears for your little ones. To help you recover from the trauma of those fears and to keep you from going completely mad, pick up a bottle of the big and bold **Stark Raving Red** from Rosenblum Cellars. The unique red color, resulting from a blend of grapes, combined with aromas of dark bing cherries and ripe, rich plums will remind you of the emergency you just survived.

The First Stitches

"At least it will be a great story when he gets older," the old gentleman quipped after we told him the huge bandage on my son's face was covering his first set of stitches. Six stitches.

That's one way to look at it! I thought.

It was the day after Christmas. My parents had visited and were going to be driving back home the following day so my mom and I decided to hit the after-Christmas sales while my husband was at work. Grandpa happily volunteered for one-on-two time with my boys. We live in a resort area, so I suggested they ride the town shuttle to the playground. Sometimes I think the boys love the shuttle more than the playground or arcade! So Grandpa announced the upcoming ride to the boys, and they ran through the house excitedly shouting, "We're going on the shuttle! We're going on the shuttle!"

My mom and I kissed the boys good-bye and set out for our morning together. By the time we'd returned—in time for me to take my dad out on our ritual lunch together–they hadn't even gotten home yet. My mom texted my dad who wrote back to say the boys had had a blast and eaten a great pizza lunch. They were now waiting for the shuttle to show up to take them home. A few minutes after boarding, my dad texted us a photo of the happy boys on the shuttle bus.

Within minutes, the front door swung open with a bang (as it often does when the boys return home from anywhere). My oldest was shouting, "Mama! Zac is hurt! He needs a Band-Aid!"

As the mother of boys, this is a common announcement around my house—I even hear it when my son stubs his toe—so it didn't make me panic. My dad handed my bawling son to me. I still didn't realize anything major was wrong until I went to clean up his scraped chin. He didn't have just a simple cut. It was deep. Thankfully, my mom was there to offer the opinion that, yes, indeed, we needed to head to the emergency room because Zac would need stitches.

Off we went! And soon enough, we were having the procedure. Zac, as brave as could be, was lying on a medical bed with a naive me holding his hand at his side. I had no idea what we were about to go through together—a mom and her baby's pain. Oh, the torture of it! I realized then exactly what my mom meant all those times when I was a child and she'd whisper to me that she wished she could take away my pain. That's all I wanted for my son: to take all his pain and fear away from him.

Zac screamed and kicked as the doctor stuck the needle in his chin. Tears flowed from his eyes. I held back my own tears, trying to keep it together for my boy. Then I was asked to hold down his arms and head. Agony! As the doctor started to stitch, I think seeing the thread and needle freaked him out because he shrieked.

Panicking, I wanted to yell at the doctor, "How do you *know* he's not feeling this?!" Apparently those words had come out of my mouth because she answered that she'd given him plenty of anesthesia. I had no choice but to believe her and have faith that it wasn't as bad as it seemed. What seemed to last for hours, but really only went on for about 20 minutes, was finally over. I kissed my son's forehead a million times and brushed his hair back and told him how brave he was. "Can we go home now? I want to go home—now," he calmly yet firmly stated.

A couple of hours and an ice cream treat later, I took my father out for a drink. What was supposed to have been our lunch had now turned into a much-needed cocktail. Though he was relieved to see how Zac was back to his 4-year-old self, full of energy, he felt terrible!

Over a piña colada and a margarita, he told me how it all went down. In a split second on the shuttle, my son stood up at the very moment it hit a speed bump. Just like that! Oh, I feel so bad for my dad and any other grandparent if a child under their care gets hurt. Truly, it could happen to any of us at any time, but when it's on their watch, everyone feels bad.

There's no blame here at all. In fact, my heart feels so many things—for my son, for my father, for my mom who was by my side, and even for my son's big brother who had to hang tough (it made him *so* upset!) through it all.

DARE TO PAIR

When the inevitable accidents of our children's lives occur, Mommy's heart skips a beat. With the soft, enticing color of fresh rose petals, the **Red Stitch Soberanes Vineyard Pinot Noir** will likely persuade you to pour more than one glass. Once you do, this wine's ripe cranberry and pomegranate aromas and its undertones of mocha and coffee will help mend mommy's wounds after a day of comforting your little one.

Our Adventure Was Truly Frightening

The coiled snake floating a mere four feet from our canoe as we set off foreshadowed the "adventure" that was coming our way. I'm quoting my husband and some friends by calling it that. For me, it was not an adventure, but more of a nightmare. Throughout it, I just wanted to burst into tears and be back, safe, in my home, far, far away from nature and *adventure.*

Three of my friends and their families (16 of us in total) boarded canoes for a four-hour excursion down the Econfina River in Florida. During the first sunny hour we discovered a crystal clear, sandy-bottomed spring to explore along one bank of the river. We tied up our canoes so we could frolic in the refreshing spring water. After lunch, we settled back in our canoes and meandered down the river through a tunnel of oak-and-palm forests, the sun intermittently breaking through the canopy of the treetops. In the distance, we could hear the romantic rumbling of thunder, but there was no rain—yet.

The escalating drumbeat of thunder was making me nervous, but it still sounded pretty far away, and blue skies were still right above us. Our cell phones didn't work so we couldn't check the weather forecast, yet it was clear the storm was getting closer. Up ahead, I noticed a couple waving us to stay right.

"Snake!" they shouted.

My heart was starting to pound. We steered past the danger only for our next peril to begin—rain. And the thunder was getting louder and scarier.

The end of our route wasn't for another mile, which meant it was a good hour away. Worse, there were no more springs with covered picnic areas along the river's path so there was nowhere to take shelter, just a few houses along the way with "Private Property"and "No Trespassing" signs nailed to several trees. One friend suggested we beach our canoes and take cover at one such property. But, in my mind, I didn't know which was worse: living out a scene from *Deliverance* or a full-on, overhead thunderstorm. A couple of families chose this option while eight of us continued on.

After some time of hearing thunder, we saw our first streak of lightning. With panic overriding my every rational thought, all I could imagine was a tree would be struck and land on one of us. I turned to look behind me at my husband who was fiercely paddling. My wonderful five-year-old son looked concerned.

"I want to go home *now!*" he declared.

The rumbling kept on. Then a bright flash of light. A crack. Then, crash! We pulled the canoes over at an embankment along a bend in the river. Just an hour ago, we had been sur-rounded by people on the river, passing us, laughing, drink-ing, and playing. Now—there wasn't a single soul. It was the eight of us and God. OMG! I pulled my youngest son onto my lap. He curled into a ball and I cuddled him tight. My five-year-old was behind me crying. I wanted him in my arms too, but there wasn't enough room at the bow. I yelled back to my hus-band to hold our son,. "He needs to be comforted!" Another flash. Soon there was only minutes between violent crashes of thunder. I wanted to cry. Or throw up. I began to pray.

Under no circumstances did I want my children to see the fear in my eyes or hear the panic in my voice. I looked over at the canoe next to ours at my friend and her three children (her husband was at work). She was smiling and every time the thunder would rock our world, she'd raise her arms up, clap and yell out, "Woooo! Now *that* was a good one! *This* is an adventure children!" Her kids smiled up at her, believing her.

At that moment I decided I had to change my attitude. I began to sing into my youngest's ear, songs I used to sing when he was a baby. I continued until the rain lightened up and we decided to paddle again. As we made our way down the river to the spot where our shuttle was waiting, I was still a bit tense. Then blue skies started to peek out from behind the clouds and the rain completely stopped. We heard whooping and hollering behind us and looked upriver to see that the other two families had caught up with us. They'd spent the storm in a shed full of chickens—and no loners with shotguns had turned up. We were all safe and happy to be reunited.

On the shuttle ride back to our cars, all the children sat and laughed together. Meanwhile the adults, friends and strangers alike, chuckled in relief that we had just survived a truly frightening experience—or rather, *adventure*.

DARE TO PAIR

As parents, we often have to pretend that all is well for the sake of our kids—even when we're frightened ourselves. Luckily, the aromas of crisp pear and honey blossom, and the flavor of mango in the **Rainstorm Pinot Gris** will quickly bring you to a place of calm after the storm. Spicy and intense, this white wine is loaded with Gravenstein apple, cut pear, and a taste of orange peel.

My Son Was Born with a Heart Defect

Our son, Carter Johnson, was born June 26th 2008. As excited as we were for the arrival of our healthy baby, it wasn't long before concern set in. A small heart murmur was found during Carter's initial checkup at the hospital so the doctor ordered more tests. While heart murmurs occur quite frequently in newborn babies, they usually go away.

Just as we were getting ready to head home, Dr. Paul came in for the final check-up. We could tell by the look on his face that something was wrong. The tests had come back showing Carter had a coarctation of the aorta. COA is when the aorta is narrowed so that the amount of oxygen that the blood can pump to the lower part of the body is restricted.

We were then told our child needed a "flight for life"—be airlifted—to another hospital in Denver. My husband and I watched as a miracle unfolded into something terrible, something no parent wants to go through. In a matter of minutes, our emotions soared from happy and excited and dropped right down to sad, angry, confused, and scared.

The stress was amplified when we were given the choice of who would fly with our son? Only one of us could go: my husband or me. We didn't know what to do but ultimately decided to let the nurses and doctors do their job and that my husband and I would stay together and drive the three-hour stretch from our hometown to Denver. That decision would become one of my biggest regrets. I should have been on that flight with my son.

We hurried home, packed our clothes, and started our journey through the mountain passes to Children's Hospital in Denver. Our nightmare only got worse when we realized that the Glenwood Canyon, at the very beginning of our trek, was closed due to a bad accident. Unbelievable!

Traffic was completely backed up. In situations like this, it can be hours upon hours before things start to move again. Wanting to cry, I wasn't sure I had any tears left. We decided that we didn't care if we got a ticket or went to jail; we needed to get past all that traffic and get to our baby boy. We drove down the middle of the road, weaving in and out as necessary. Crazily enough, when we stopped to explain our situation to one of the highway transportation workers, it turned out we knew him. He was the father of a girl who'd managed a basketball team I'd coached. He happily made a few calls on our behalf. Divine intervention? Most definitely.

He told us we had permission to proceed, but with flashers on and not above 30 miles per hour. We made it through the accident and were on our way again. It still took three-and-a-half hours to get to the hospital, which felt like days.

We checked in and went right to the children's cardiac intensive care unit. Carter had his own room and was perfectly fine in his little crib. We stayed in the hospital with him that first night. I have to admit that a nurse had to tell me to stop obsessing over his heart monitor, listening for every beep. I couldn't help myself. It was a long first night.

The next day, the doctor informed us they would be doing surgery the next day. Not open-heart, but they would go in from the side to cut out the obstruction of the aorta. During the course of the two-and-a-half-hour surgery, Dr. David Campbell, Carter's heart surgeon, discovered that Carter not only had a bicuspid aortic valve but also pulmonary hypertension, meaning that the blood vessels leading to and through his lungs were also narrowed so his blood pressure was high. They left the aortic valve—something many people live with. However, because we live at a high altitude in the mountains, where the air is thinner, we would have to deal with the pulmonary hypertension.

Enter Dr. Dunbar Ivy. He informed us that Carter would have to be on oxygen and Viagra until he grew out of the condition. If he didn't, he'd have to stay on Oxygen. *Viagra*, really? He also informed us that we couldn't go home until his blood pressure came down. After many ups and downs, Carter's blood pressure finally normalized enough so we could go home, but he still had to be on oxygen 24/7 and given medication three times a day. By that time, we were exhausted, though thankful to see a light at the end of the tunnel and to be able to bring our baby boy home.

We were able to take Carter off the oxygen and Viagra when he was two. At age six, he had his second surgery. This was an open-heart surgery to deal with a subaortic stenosis. Because it was causing pressure on the aortic valve, the doctors need to scrape it out.

Preparing for open-heart surgery brought me back to day one of our journey—the fear, the anxiety, not knowing what to expect, wanting it to be over, but scared for it to start. Carter not only survived his ordeal, but has thrived. Kids are resilient, often more so than we adults. We don't give them enough credit for their strength or ability to be brave in even the scariest and most life-threatening of situations.

Unfortunately, there are many babies born with heart defects each year. I'm grateful to the nurses, the doctors, and my family who were there for Carter, my husband, and me. I thank God for the blessing of a healthy and happy little boy—every day of my life.

DARE TO PAIR

It's the most beautiful time in your entire life: you're about to bring your newborn baby home. You are excited and scared at the same time. So many mixed emotions–fear, worry, joy, all at once. There will be good times; there may be tough times. Try to persevere and lift a glass of this bold, intensely deep **Gnarly Head Old Vine Zinfandel**, with its dark-berry flavors and layers of spice, plum, pepper, and vanilla. It's the perfect toast to never giving up.

I Couldn't Save My Son from the McDonald's Slide

I'm lovin' it! On this hot, spring afternoon in South Carolina, I am, in fact, *not* loving it. Actually, I didn't mind it until my two-year-old son got stuck in the enclosed, spiral slide at McDonald's. (If you are already thinking I'm a bad mom for feeding my kid crap food, feel free to proceed to "My Fast-Food Philosophy Flew the Coop" in Chapter 7.)

It didn't occur to me that trouble could befall a child in such a wonderland. As I was chatting with my parents, I hear what sounds like Carol Ann from *Poltergeist* summoning me from the TV: "Help me. Mommy, where are you? I can't see you." I realize it's actually my little boy, who is somewhere at the top of the slide tube, which looks like a multicolored piece of the Alaskan pipeline, but I can't see him.

"Mommy's right here, baby, just slide down!" I yell up. (Come into the light, I'm thinking.) I still can hear him; and now there is fear in his voice. It's my turn to panic.

"I'm going in!" I tell my parents, doing my best imitation of Dr. Meredith Grey. *Stat.*

I slither up two turns as the heat and bad air envelop me. I can't help but think that this must be what it's like to be a tapeworm, navigating the crevices of human intestines. Even this nauseating image doesn't break my concentration. All I hear are the sobs of my first-born echoing through the tunnel. *I* want to cry. I can't breathe. I can't go up any further. The very hips that helped me push that beautiful life out into the world are the same damn ones obstructing me from helping him!

Someone help *me!* I think of moms who have fought off intruders or jumped in front of a train, the ones who have held their bare hands to their child's gushing wounds. And I can't retrieve my child from an effing slide? What's *wrong* with me, besides the fact that I might need a truckload of Vaseline to pry me out of this thing? Disappointed in myself and scared for my son, I wiggle out of the entrance of the *fun* zone. No lube necessary.

I look at my parents. Has he not come down? Should I grab an employee—who must surely be trained as a medic—to scale the steep slide to save my son? Should I try again to climb through the kiddie tunnel of hell? All I can think about was my son's fear. Can he even see us? Can he breathe? Was he thinking that he was trapped for life? That he'd never again see his loving mommy and daddy? Will he need a therapist? Will I?

Right when I thought I would vomit, a seven-year-old girl calls down to me, "I found him. He's okay!" Seconds later, she wiggles down the slide, almost skillfully, pulling my son by his ankle behind her.

DARE TO PAIR

Even Iron Man would get sweaty palms at the thought of rescuing a child from a playground tube slide. When things have gone wrong and anxiety seems to have been your main feeling all day, calm yourself with this refreshing white. Containing a touch of honeydew melon and pear with a hint of star fruit, Mouton Noire's **Knock on Wood Chardonnay** will surely set the stage for a better tomorrow.

Learning to Check My Fears

How did I picture preschool for my child? Just like everything else I imagine: all happy-go-lucky, with roses and sugar-coated cherries on top. Don't we all picture our children's lives this way? In other words, their lives will be perfect. We are going to be the best parents, have the smartest children, and the greatest home lives. And then, when reality hits, we don't know what went wrong.

I dropped Callie off for her first day of preschool with a grin on my face and a tear in my eye. How had we gotten here already? That afternoon, when I picked her up, I was given a follow-up letter telling me how wonderful my little girl is and how much happiness and enthusiasm she contributed to the group that day. My brain registered a mental check mark for a parenting success scored.

Weeks later, my daughter's pretty blonde teacher met me at the school door with the kind of smile on her face that makes me suspicious. "Callie is such an addition to our group, so charming and full of life . . . but . . ."

Oh, God.

The teacher proceeded to tell me in a no-less-bubbly manner that my daughter was having some trouble listening and had been caught telling a lie as well as stealing. Already, a young criminal on my hands.

I drove home in tears. My bad parenting had surely led to a future drug-abuser, jail-bird sociopath, and possibly worse. What was I to do?

After the opening ceremony to my pity party, a good friend convinced me that stealing a sea shell and lying about hitting a boy didn't mean that my daughter was becoming a future menace to society. She was simply typical of all other four-year-olds—she was finding herself and learning about the do's and don'ts of being a preschooler. Just because I'd let her watch too many episodes of *SpongeBob* and even *Jurassic Park* in her dinosaur-loving days didn't mean I was a terrible parent.

It's inevitable that our worry and fear will present itself at every stage of our children's evolution. Not only do we of course worry *for* and *about* our children, we also worry way too much about our adequacy as parents. Often, our expectation of ourselves are what set us up for feeling we've failed. When we don't reach the impossible goals we've set for ourselves, we become plagued by fear that we're doing parenting *wrong* and that our children will pay some kind of price for it.

Callie is thriving in preschool now. It took some time, but we eventually worked past the small issues she was having and have since moved on. I had to realize: she's only four. We're going to have *many* more hurdles in the future! I just need to stay out of my own fears about myself and keep my perspective by talking to other moms. That way, I won't waste any more precious time on fears that I'm failing my kids.

DARE TO PAIR

Bringing to mind the power and beauty of horses jumping hurdles in equestrian sports, the richly textured **Black Stallion Estate Chardonnay** is made from grapes grown in several regions, each contributing unique layers of complexity. Sometimes we moms may not be as graceful as we'd like in tackling the stumbling blocks that life inevitably sends our way, especially once our worries and fears about ourselves become activated. On those days, the bright lemon zest of this wine, along with its nose of green apple, hazelnut, and a lovely hint of vanilla cream soda, will remind you to relax—you *are* a champion.

CHAPTER 5
Stressed to the Max

*T*ugged in so many different directions most of the time, we moms become quite accustomed to stress. We know that the things that push us over the edge don't necessarily come in waves; they hit you all at once like a tsunami. Is there anything more daunting than flying with babies? Or the endless nights of colic? It's the extreme situations, compounded by our already stressed lives that push us beyond even a *mother's* capacity to deal.

Once the dust has settled, dealing with the trauma sometimes requires less talking and more sipping, which is why we happily pour the vino in lieu of seeking out a therapist.

Baby-Making is Making Me Crazy

All of the articles and Internet posts I read about the signs of early pregnancy put sore boobs at the top of the list. So just a few days after I was late, I poked my girls thinking, *do they hurt?* (Now, if you are a member of the going-crazy-while-trying-to-conceive club, you know very well what the acronym DTD stands for, or you may have just figured it out. DTD is Doing the Dance—otherwise known as sex. In fact, whether you are new to the game or have been around the block a few times, you probably know that the process of conception is littered with acronyms, so I'll be sure to define them all.)

How about now? and I poked again. I'm 11 DPO (Days Past Ovulation) in my TWW (Two Week Wait) and my boobs were very sore. But I couldn't tell if they were sore because I was expecting or because I couldn't stop harassing them.

I didn't realize, until now, that trying to conceive could make a woman so *nuts!*

I'll admit I'm a lucky woman. I already have two handsome, amazing sons. To have my boys, we just went off birth control and let nature take its course. After just two months, my oldest was conceived. There was no obsessing, no charting, no temperature taking—no craziness. I woke up one morning, realized AF (Aunt Flow, your period) had never come and, voilà, I was pregnant! My son was six-months-old when I found out I was pregnant again. The only sign then was that I just didn't feel "normal." When I did the test, I was already eight-weeks pregnant. There's no pregnancy-related acronym that I know of for that surprise.

My husband and I had always talked about going for a third child. Then at a certain point, I felt as though I was ready to try. So I told him, and he climbed on board the baby-making train (figuratively and literally). And since I wasn't getting any younger, I signed up for this crazy game of TTC (Trying to Conceive). Trust me, it *is* a game. A game that is supposed to be fun, but somehow turns into an addiction, yet the only rehab is a BFP (Big Fat Positive—you're pregnant!).

I bought a basal thermometer (which comes with a handy-dandy chart) and bookmarked BabyCenter's ovulation calculator. At first, I was fairly certain it'd take just one try so we only DTDed once during the 48 hours prior to my supposed ovulation date. Afterwards, I propped my backside up on a couple of pillows and lay in a 90-degree angle for two episodes of *Friends* reruns. I *knew* we had just made a baby.

And then the obsession began.

Every single twinge of pain or discomfort sent me into a tizzy. *Is that a sign? What about that?* As I got closer to 10 DPO (Days Past Ovulation), I found myself typing into Google "10 DPO symptoms," then scanning symptoms for an hour, and looking for the announcement of a BFP by every woman who had had the same symptoms as me. I'd only feel satisfied when someone reported feeling the way I was and disheartened when they didn't list any of my symptoms. Taking my temperature, checking my CM (Cervical Mucous)—it all became a regular part of my day during that two week waiting period. *No pun intended.*

When AF came four days later than expected, I was bummed, but ready to take the challenge *again!* I bought an OPK (Ovulation Predictor Kit) and used all seven tests until I saw that beaming smiley face that might as well have said out loud, *"You got this one girl—go grab your man!"* Of course, with two boys running around the house, we had to wait. Finally, the boys were nestled all snug in their beds, while visions of sweet lovin' danced in our heads. We did it. And just like in *Groundhog Day* where Bill Murray's character finds himself reliving a day in his life over and over again, I found myself lying propped on my pillows, watching *Friends* reruns. I even grabbed my iPhone and watched BabyCenter's fertilization video, *seriously.* I think I watched it twice, believing I had started the process that begins a new life. And my daydreams began, *again.*

I would walk by a dumpster and feel nauseated by the smell. *"That's totally a symptom; why else would that smell so bad to me!"*

"I am craving food like crazy." *Couldn't be that I skipped dinner the night before.*

"I'm irritable when my husband complains about wasting food." *"Doesn't that always make me irritable?"* But when you're TTC, you can turn almost every single moment into a *sign.*

At 11 DPO, I felt crampy and had spotting. I knew that AF was on her way and I texted the only friend I was talking to about this. *"Oh no!"* I wrote. She convinced me to wait it out. It ain't over until AF actually arrives.

The waiting.

Tick tock. Two weeks *never* felt so long.

DTD, pray, *test.* Wash, rinse, *repeat.*

If you get a BFN (Big Fat Negative—bummer, not pregnant!), you have to wait *two* more weeks to try again and then two *more* weeks to find out. This world of TTC is maddening and not for the weak of heart, but babies are *worth it.*

If you do have to play the game, have fun with it and try not to become obsessed. Remember, stress affects conception. Or, maybe I just read that. Good luck to you!

DARE TO PAIR

When you're getting the baby-making blues, a lovely glass of **Sexual Chocolate California Blend**, from Slo Down Vineyards, will ease your stress. Bursting with intense flavors of blackberry, black cherry, dark chocolate and spice with a delicate, smooth finish—this wine will have you ready to try, try again.

There's a New Level of Helplessness When Mommy is Sick

When your child is sick, especially when it's your infant, you feel as if life couldn't get much worse. That's what I felt like when a stomach bug hit our house—and hit it *hard*. My two-year-old son was the first to start vomiting. Of course, it began as most childhood sicknesses do, at around one in the morning.

With a new baby in the house, we'd recently moved our toddler to a big-boy bed. He took to sleeping in it relatively well—after my husband or I would read 10-plus books to him and sing him to sleep! Of course there were a few nights each week when he would stealthily tiptoe into our bedroom and crawl in our bed. But one particular night was different. Jakob was crying wearily from his bedroom, and my mental rendition of the ABCs, which I used to time how long I'd let him cry, ended with him still sobbing.

I found him still in his bed, tears running down his cheeks, with puke all over. It was in his hair, eyelashes, and streaked down his bare chest. His pillow, sheets, and comforter were all splattered. I scooped up his little 25-pound body and took him to rinse in the tub. Not knowing what was coming next, I dressed him in fresh PJs and brought him to bed with us.

Ten peaceful minutes slipped by before his chest began heaving and another round of vomit found its way into another bed. This time there wasn't nearly as much, and my husband cleaned up Jakob while I stripped and remade the bed (much appreciation to whoever invented the waterproof mattress cover.)

This time around, we were savvier. We left Jakob in only his diaper and placed a large puke bucket right next to the bed. Four more rounds of puking that night equaled not much sleep for anyone, especially, since the baby's routine was to wake up at 5:00 a.m. to nurse.

But my husband made it to work that day like a champ, while I went into proficient zombie-mommy mode. In the same fashion that my mom did for us when we were little and sick, I made Jakob a sick bed on the couch, surrounded him with crayons and coloring books, an empty ice cream bucket, and turned on cartoons. Big, empty ice cream buckets have many super-clever uses, one of them being they make excellent puke buckets. You can rinse and reuse them after the little jobs; and simply snap on the lid and toss the ones you can't stomach yourself.

Jakob stopped throwing up around noon that day. It had been quite the challenge trying to keep him hydrated since he'd throw up water after 10 minutes of drinking it. But during lunch time he kept down a whole Pedialyte popsicle, and things started to look up. I think I even managed a nap that day in between the piles of laundry, but honestly the details are a little fuzzy.

Things were "fairly normal" and that night the plan was dinner, a movie and to bed early. As we dined that evening on a simple dinner of chicken noodle soup, the baby started vomiting. My kids all spit up after nursing. I tried a lot of techniques to prevent it, but still they spit. This was different. A 4-month-old was projectile vomiting from the swing where he was cradled while we ate.

I held my baby over the sink (holding an infant over a dirty toilet was not an option) three more times that evening. More heaping piles of laundry, a hard wooden rocking chair, and the uneasy feeling that this was not over kept me company through the night. Dozing off and on in the boys room, I wasn't exactly aware of what time my husband was afflicted.

Sometime during the wee morning hours, he was struck with the same stomach bug and ended up "sleeping" on the bathroom floor. That is where I found him early the next morning when I went to take a shower to wash off the nighttime infant vomit.

Another day passed with me looking like someone straight out of The *Walking Dead*, this time likely a mommy less proficient. I had a rambunctious healthy toddler and demanding, still not back-to-normal baby, plus a sick man down for the day. As my dad would say, men have bigger muscles than their soft-skinned counterparts so, when afflicted with a sickness where your body aches like the flu, their bodies ache *infinitely* more. Sigh.

Details of the next day are obviously a little more fuzzy, but they included another 10 loads of laundry (couch cushions, mattress-pad covers, comforters, and every single towel we owned), light meals (not the most fun way to lose weight), water deliveries to "the master sick room," and—did I mention nursing every three hours? Luckily we were stocked on groceries (not that we were eating much) and so we quarantined ourselves for day two.

That night I slept on the couch so that I could put a little distance between my sick man and me under the pretense that I wanted *him* to get a good night's sleep. It worked! The next morning I woke up from six hours of uninterrupted sleep feeling the best I had in two days. My husband got up and went to work feeling at least well rested if not yet a hundred percent himself. Both boys had their appetites and shining smiles back and the sun was blazing in a clear blue sky. I could have even envisioned bluebirds on my shoulder.

Silly me—this was not to last. As I was in the middle of catching up on an entire counter full of dirty dishes, my turn arrived. I managed to grab my phone before escaping to the bathroom where, knowing what was coming, I called my sister. Interrupted by tears from boys waking up from their naps, I crawled upstairs and comforted them as much as possible before scurrying back to the bathroom. Just before my sister arrived, as I had my head in the toilet with a two-year-old crying on my leg and an infant bawling in the next room, I was reminded of the thought I had had the day before while I was holding the baby over the sink. *"This couldn't get much worse!"* But, oh had it!

When Mommy is sick, there is a new level of helplessness. At least when the members of my family were sick I could comfort them, wait on them, and shower them with unconditional love even while cleaning their puke out of my cleavage. Yet when I'm sick, the world might as well just stop. No one is cleaning up after me or preparing a snack for the healthy kids. There's no homemade chicken-noodle soup or refilled water glasses and no picking up a crying baby or reading stories to the toddler.

DARE TO PAIR

Cleaning up everyone else's puke is punishment enough, you'd think. However when sickness has traveled around your house fast enough to have Mommy begging for her own time-out, keep in mind that, when things die down, you can turn to this delicate yet fruity **Mommy's Time Out Delicious Red**. With a silky texture and smooth, sensuous aroma, this wine is sure to give you the break you no doubt need.

Luckily for me, my sister is aunt extraordinaire! The 15 minutes it took her to get to my house felt like an hour, but it was followed by eight hours of peacefulness. After purging everything my stomach had to give, I pulled the blackout drapes against the sunny blue sky and slept the best sleep I had had in days!

Flying Cross-Country with Two Kids Under Two

It seems as if everyone has a "you're not going to believe this actually happened" story. Ours began as we were leaving California, after spending three months there with our two children, ages one and two.

We had to be at the airport for our journey home at quarter to five in the morning. Sometime while we'd been away, the air carrier had changed its gate-check policy so we weren't allowed to check our stroller at the gate, but had to check it as luggage. Having our stroller would have been a huge help at each of the three airports on our itinerary. But, we had no choice but to check it along with our nine bags of luggage and two car seats. In hindsight, this was the first omen. *Not* a good one.

We flew from Monterey, California to Los Angeles. After a bit of a rocky start, the rest of the morning seemed to go without a hitch as we flew on to Atlanta. While in Atlanta waiting for the flight that was the last leg of our trip home to Florida, we discovered that the flight was delayed an hour. We looked at this as sort of a blessing since it gave us time to sit down for a meal at the airport. Little did we know, it would be our last for a long while.

Our flight continued to be delayed with each passing hour—the Atlanta airport is known for being the world's, yes, the *world's* busiest airport. My patience was beginning to fray and we missed our stroller even more. Admittedly, I'm a bit of a germaphobe so I was well aware that every square inch of the Atlanta airport is probably filled with germs, dirt and unknown ickiness. Yet, reflecting my increasingly frazzled state of mind, I began to let my children roll around on the filthy, stained carpets, frolicking in the germs. And worst of all, I'm pretty sure my one-year-old ate some unknown—let's hope it was food—item off the floor while crawling underneath the seats in the waiting area. (Rest assured, hand sanitizer is permanently in my clear-plastic quart-sized carry-on baggie when I travel now.)

Suddenly, the gate agent disappeared, and the *real* trouble began. First, the announcement: our flight was canceled. My husband, a seasoned traveler, was immediately on the phone to secure us a rental car to drive home. I thought he was crazy! We couldn't possibly drive home. We didn't have our car seats or three-month's worth of luggage. I urged him to go to another line with a new gate agent to get us placed on a different flight home. It turned out that, because it was the July fourth weekend, the next available flight wasn't for three days!

By this point, the kids were light-years past their bedtimes. When we requested that our bags be released to us, the baggage handler laughed at us. He told us it would take at least four hours. (Little did he know, our bags had made it onto the next flight and were already in Florida.)

It was around 11 p.m. when we headed out to pick up our rental car. When my husband had called to secure the rental, hoping to save time, he'd requested that car seats be installed and ready to go. After waiting in yet another line, we were assured that the car seats were installed. With keys in hand, we set off to locate the car.

Of course, it was in the farthest corner of a dark, cavernous parking garage; and, while our son who was being carried was too tired to care, our daughter refused to walk another step in the terrifying garage. With my daughter now safe in her daddy's arms, we finally made it to the car, only to find—no car seats. We found them in the trunk, but they were brand-new so we had to remove their shrink-wraps before we could install them ourselves.

My exhausted husband struggled to install the seats in the dark, unable to read the instructions. When he told me to just buckle the kids into the back seat, sit in-between them and hold onto them, I became seriously worried about my husband—also known as "Safety Todd."

I immediately suggested we find the nearest hotel, get some rest, and head home in the morning. A short drive later, bone weary from traveling and hanging out at the airport for six hours, we staggered onto the hotel elevator about midnight. Three very mischievous boys slid into the elevator with us just before the doors closed. It was obvious they were with the numerous traveling baseball teams who were running wild around the hotel. One ill-advised boy hit every single floor's button on the elevator so the whole ride we stopped at *every single floor.*

All we wanted was to collapse into bed so a part of me didn't have the heart to tell my husband that we were literally down to one last diaper when we got into our hotel room. As both kids were still in diapers, I had to break the news to him. While I bathed the kids, my exhausted husband ventured out to see if he could find a store open after midnight that sold diapers, toothbrushes, and other necessities. I put the baby in the last diaper, pleaded with our daughter to *not* "go potty" in the room, and prayed not only for my husband's safety in that sketchy run-down part of town, but also his sanity. Eventually, he returned with all our supplies and we got some much needed rest. The next day we hit the road—with car seats properly installed.

Many families have a trip-from-hell story that they look back on with laughter and jokes years later. I, on the other hand, still cringe at the mere thought of that trip, and am grateful I've never had to go through that kind of experience again.

DARE TO PAIR

When it comes to flying with young children, it's almost guaranteed you'll need to pour a glass of wine upon arrival at your destination—whether or not it's the place you intended to be. With **Fifth Leg Chardonnay**—and its notes, which include the bright fruits guava and peach, along with a crisp, lively palate of crunchy Granny Smith apples and later a citrus finish—you'll soar above your troubles.

My Son Fell Out of a Second Story Window

I love spring. I enjoy all the seasons, actually, but I'm always ready for winter to be over and spring to unfold. I thrive on the renewed energy that the early days of spring deliver. It's the feeling you get on that first warm day when the snow has nearly all melted, the sun is illuminating a crystal blue sky, and the mercury has risen enough to throw open the windows for the first time in months.

That was exactly the kind of day I woke to on what was to be the worst day of my life. With two little boys and a baby on the way, winter had been a bit cluttered and claustrophobic in our home. Rejoicing in the opportunity to let in fresh air, I cracked the windows and commenced a thorough spring cleaning.

My oldest son had just celebrated his third birthday and was happily playing in the second-story toy room with his 14-month-old brother. I was vacuuming enough dog hair out of the carpet to weave a jacket in the adjacent hallway. To this day, I'm not exactly sure what made me turn my head, but I did turn just in time to see that the room's window was wide open and the screen was missing. Only the baby was in the room. This was the first of a series of horrible images permanently imprinted on my brain that day.

In a matter of half a second, as my brain took in the scene, I realized what had happened. If I had been hooked up to an EEG at that moment, I may have been pronounced dead because I'm sure my heart stopped beating. But during the second half of that second, I sprang into action. I dropped the vacuum and launched over the baby gate, barreling down the stairs two or three at a time, and out the front door. On the concrete driveway lay my three-year-old son, Jakob, surrounded by blood and whimpering.

The blood was pooled around his head. I bent down to him urgently reassuring him that "Mommy's here, Mommy's here, Oh, Mommy is here!" That's when I heard my youngest son crying upstairs and I knew that I had to go to him to avoid a repeat situation. I urgently, yet carefully, scooped up Jakob and carried him in the front door and laid him down on the floor. (While I have been trained not to move head injury victims, that thought didn't cross my mind. I knew I had to do whatever I needed to do to protect my babies and get it done quickly.)

It felt as if I was moving at superhero speed through all of this. I sprinted to the kitchen, grabbed my phone, and started the 911 call. Then I flew up the stairs and gathered up my crying baby, tucking him under my arm like a football and returned to Jakob. At this point I was trying to keep Jakob still on the floor, but he was crying and thrashing around. Blood was everywhere.

As for the 911 call, I was able to give the dispatcher the necessary information all in one breath, but breathing was not my priority. She calmly stayed on the line issuing reassurances as I delivered orders to Jakob to: "Stay awake. Stay with me honey!" By the time that the emergency responders arrived only several minutes had passed. The image of me crouched over Jakob, my baby still tucked under my arm, and all three of us in tears welcomed them to the scene.

With great urgency, the paramedics examined Jakob and promptly put him in a tiny neck brace. When he started to drift off to sleep, I renewed my pleading to "stay awake," but the female medic kindly told me it was okay for him to sleep because it was his body's way of dealing with the pain. I took a small step back; and one of the paramedics offered to call my husband. My husband recalls that as the worst phone conversation of his life.

In very little time, Jakob was on a stretcher and escorted out to an ambulance while one of the generous firefighters was holding my baby. He asked if he could be the one to bring the baby to the hospital, and I agreed, trusting him. I rode in the front of the ambulance as there were two medics working with Jakob in the back. Although we didn't have too far to go, my husband beat us there. I fell into his arms as the paramedics carried Jakob inside, who was crying more forcefully now— which I took as a good sign.

My husband and I stood in the background of the emergency room to allow the team of doctors and nurses to do their jobs. Not speaking, we just stood there holding hands. At the first break in the action, we would jump right to Jakob's side. I held his precious little hand and bent over him so he could see my face. He was talking now between sobs, and only I could understand what he was saying. He wanted the brace off and for me to hold him.

When the portable X-ray machine was wheeled in, a sympathetic nurse came to my side and asked if there was any chance that I was pregnant. Until that moment, I hadn't thought for one second about me, my body, or my pregnancy. But I *was* twelve weeks pregnant. She gently took my arm and stood in the hall with me while my husband took over as the present parent.

More X-rays, doctors' and nurses' exams, phone calls, and an MRI later, it was decided that Jakob would be transported to a larger hospital about an hour away but that our case didn't warrant a helicopter, which I took as another good sign. Before we left I had to give an official statement to a detective. Fortunately, the detective was compassionate and my interview was brief, my husband holding my hand the entire time.

In the ambulance for the transfer, I again had to ride in the front, while Jakob, bawling, was loaded in the back with a paramedic. My husband would follow in his truck after a quick stop at home to get a change of clothes for me and Jakob. There, my thoughtful brother-in-law had washed the blood off the driveway and was mopping when my husband arrived with the detective. My brother-in-law explained that he didn't want me to have to come home to see that scene. The investigation was brief and my husband was on the road.

Jakob cried most of the hour's drive to the next hospital and vomited all over in the back of the ambulance and on the paramedic. Once we were wheeled into that emergency room, I was able to soothe him into a soft whimper. My husband was back by our sides before the first doctor arrived.

After three examinations by three different doctors, another round of X-rays, and countless nurse visits, we had a diagnosis of a severe concussion and a skull fracture. Amazingly, there were no other broken bones and hardly any other bruises. We were escorted upstairs to intensive care where Jakob was to remain for monitoring and where they removed Jakob's neck brace. Now he was able to sit up in bed and there was just enough room for me to crawl in next to him.

Recently, there has been a lot of research on sports-related concussions so doctors know more about how the brain reacts, is damaged, and recovers. There are no good concussions; and we were told that concussions in children are especially concerning because their brains fill the entire skull so there is very little room for it to swell. As for the fracture above his left ear, most of the blood escaped through his ear canal—a good sign for his healing brain—but surgery still wasn't ruled out.

That night, Jakob wasn't allowed to eat and could only suck water off of a sponge. My husband had no appetite and I had a vending machine dinner of crackers and juice, which were tasteless, only because of my growing baby. After Jakob fell asleep, my husband and I talked most of the night. We tried not to dwell on the what-ifs, but they came up: what if Jakob could never hear again? What if I lost the baby? What if . . .

Mostly, though, I spent that night thinking about all that I had envisioned for my son's future and how it could be affected by the accident. How would this affect him at school, at little league, in high school football? Would his brain develop normally or would he be developmentally stuck at age three for the rest of his life? Would he ever grow up to love a woman and be blessed with a family of his own?

As the sun crept over the horizon and the hospital came alive again, Jakob was wheeled into another MRI. Impatiently I waited behind protective glass while his father held his hand. Our brave boy was so still he didn't need restraints. The promising results showed very little trauma remaining in his brain and emergency surgery was no longer imminent. More examinations (a neurosurgeon, pediatrician, and ear, nose and throat doctor made up his team) all led to our discharge early that afternoon.

With instructions to limit activities that might cause repeat concussions, we contemplated having him wear a helmet his every waking minute, but decided against it. Friends and family poured in with "quiet-time'" toys such as coloring books, movies, stickers, and candy. My mother-in-law came for a visit, which took some of the 24/7–observation burden off of me.

We had a follow-up with the ear, nose, and throat doctor and Jakob passed all his hearing tests. After a few months, we were able to relax. My pregnancy remained healthy and I delivered a beautiful baby girl six months after the accident. I cried with joy that she would be able to know Jakob and that he could be an older brother to her.

There are still days, nearly four years after Jakob's fall, that I think about all the things that I could have done to prevent it. And I don't think I'll ever forget the vivid details of some of the disturbing images from that day.

I also think about how differently that day could have turned out—what might have been the result had there been brain damage or worse. And I'll probably always worry about recurring concussions as he plays sports or he tries out for football someday. But for now and every day, I'm happy and grateful to have three healthy, boisterous, and cheerful children to love, nourish and appreciate.

DARE TO PAIR

There are days in motherhood that can scare you beyond measure. Events occur that stop you right in your normally busy, unstoppable tracks. When it turns out that you are imaginably blessed with a good outcome to a bad event, salute your luck by drinking a few glasses of this crisp white **Fall Creek Vineyards Sauvignon Blanc**. Its well-knitted aromas are laced with floral tones and it boasts a crisp acidity. One hundred percent Sauvignon Blanc, you'll find your-self savoring flavors of citrus and passion fruit and appreciating the dryness of this elegant wine.

It's My Turn to Have a Tantrum!

I've always considered myself laid-back. I was the one in college who didn't care which bar or party we went to; I was up for anything. Whenever something stressful happened, I'd always retort, "It's all good!" I've moved across the country twice, experienced ups and downs in my career, and even endured a brief split from my long-term boyfriend (now my dear husband). Sure, things would upset me, but, outwardly, I was always able to hold it in and put on a smile. Until I had children, I really didn't know my temper existed.

You know that you're having one of those days when you're so exhausted and stressed, you can just feel it. You notice that Swiper is actually pissing you off, when normally you ignore what's happening on *Dora the Explorer.* Then you find yourself in an internal debate over why Dora is always so damn nice to him when he's clearly a jerk. All this, then you suddenly realize that there is no way you will be able to accomplish half of the things you need to. There are never enough hours.

Call it the lack of me time to veg out and watch *Pretty Woman* over and over again, the being on duty 24/7, or the 20-minute frenzy it takes to prepare (going to the potty, getting dressed, the debate about whether they can bring their favorite doggie—why did he take his shoes off—car seats) for a 10-minute run to the store. Throw in the lack of sleep and even the sweetest little debutante could lose her *shizzle*.

I was truly at the end of my rope, although trying to keep it together. I'd taken advantage of the rainy day to clean the house. My final touch was picking up all the toys right before nap time, which always leaves me with a wonderful sense of calm as I enjoy some quiet while the kids are asleep. In fact, I was counting the minutes to that time. Maybe I'd order a movie from pay-per-view and really relax.

Just as I started to usher my two boys into their room for their naps, my three-year-old grabbed an entire box of cars and planes and dumped it all over the living room floor in one loud crash!

Enter: mommy tantrum.

"Why? Why, why—*why?!* Why would you do that?" I scream, with tears in my eyes. "I just cleaned up this whole room. We have to take a nap, you *know* this. Why would you do that?"

He blankly stares at me as I fall to my knees and start slamming each and every Matchbox vehicle back into the blue plastic container.

"I don't understand why you'd do that. Do you *like* to watch me pick up toys? Do you *like* for me to have no time for myself?"

DARE TO PAIR

Sometimes just a lot of little things can add up to a big pile of-stress, especially when our most-hoped for expectations are dashed. Perfect for those days when you've had a meltdown, try **Sweet Bitch Merlot**. This red has a little sweetness that rounds out the taste and brings out the blackberry, raspberry, and vanilla flavors. It will help you get past the feeling that you're at the end of your rope.

Now, he's really lost as I'm going on about nonsense. Frazzled, I start to cry. Then I realize it could be damaging for him to see me like this, so I grab and hug him tight, apologizing for yelling at him.

"It's okay, Mommy. I'm sorry."

My heart aches that he apologized for such a simple offense.

"I love you so much, baby. Mommy is just tired. Let's all take a nap and then I'll give you and your brother a special treat when you wake up." After I put the kiddos to bed and leave the room, I collapse on the couch and cry all the stress of the day out. And then—I nap, too.

I Feel the Darkness of Motherhood Enveloping Me

She's screaming again. How can she be awake already? I fed her only an hour ago. But, sure enough—she's screaming. I wait in dread for two minutes to see if she stops so precious silence can ensue, but it doesn't. I look over at my husband sleeping peacefully next to me. Of course he's sleeping; it isn't his night. I rip the covers back in irritation. Last night was his night, and he only had to get up twice. It's 2:00 a.m., and I've been up four times already.

Sighing, I stomp toward my three-month-old's room. I know I need to let go of this anger; she's going to sense it and it won't help the situation at all. The wails only get louder as I approach the room, and when I enter, I see her flailing her arms around, her little face scrunched up in agony. I pick her up, and hold her writhing body next to mine. I feel my heart start racing, the anxiety and frustration no doubt building.

It's her colic—again. Her tummy hurts. I rock and sing, trying to soothe her, but my heart isn't in it; and she knows it. She screams louder, begging for my true attention. I try, but it's just not there. I'm exhausted, I have to work tomorrow, but why would she care? I try to remember that she's the baby, I'm the adult, and she's in pain. I attempt her pacifier, which she's never really been into—she's a thumb sucker—and she's not having it. She only cries louder.

I rock back and forth, clenching my teeth as she wails. I watch the door, wondering if my husband will hear us and get out of bed to come help me. I'm not even sure at this point what he would do, or why I'm even so angry at him, but I am. I know I've been taking all my frustration out on him. He's experiencing this nightmare right with me, this I know. However I can't help but feel resentment every night on my way home from work. If he forgets to put his dishes in the dishwasher, or leaves the toilet seat up. Every single thing irritates me, and it never used to be like this. I wonder how long this phase will last, hoping that it is indeed, a phase. I stare at the door, but no one comes to rescue me.

It's so dark. I try to imagine myself on a beach somewhere, soaking in the rays and drinking a margarita. I get up and walk, patting her on the back as I pace, back and forth. Slowly I hear her starting to calm—the crying stops and short, labored breathing begins. She starts to relax, laying her head on my shoulder. I sit back down in the rocking chair slowly, not wanting to wake her now. Exhausted, she gives up, eventually falling into a deep slumber.

I know I have so much to be thankful for. Overall, our baby is healthy. I am married, and have a husband that is pretty helpful, compared to most. I have a job that helps pay the bills, and while I miss our little girl while I'm away, the escape during this trying time truly helps. What doesn't help is that the doctor can't tell us what's truly wrong, or even what we can do to help her. It seems colic is the catch-all term for babies who cry incessantly or have consistent tummy aches. Not to mention, I don't feel like myself. I'm not sure if it's the constant ring of crying, my new body...or my hormones; but lately I've felt so sad. I didn't even want to think about the word depression, or meds that would help with that. Heck, I can barely take a shower or go the bathroom. Every lunch break I have is spent grocery shopping, or running errands to avoid taking a crying baby to the store. I can't imagine adding another thing to the list. I know everyone keeps saying it will get better, and I know it will. It just appears this new thing I call being a mom isn't as shiny on the inside, as it was presented on the outside.

I watch her eyelids flutter a bit, and am thankful when they don't open. I gaze at her a few minutes longer, relishing seeing her so peaceful. I kiss my baby girl on the forehead as I lay her down in her crib, and creep quietly back to my room. Tomorrow is a new day. And while it will be another hard day, I know that I am strong enough to get through these tough times. Even more importantly, that down the road, they will merely be a flicker of a memory.

DARE TO PAIR

Whether it's the frustration of colic or just life hitting you all at once, remember you are in good company. Some mom somewhere has been where you are. After the little one is tucked in tight, savor some of **The Dark Side of the Moon Cabernet Sauvignon**, from Wines That Rock, and say a toast to the travails of mothers everywhere. With aromas of black currant and cherry, followed by rich flavors of cassis, toasted vanilla beans, and hints of chocolate—this dry red wine is sure to lighten even the blackest of nights.

CHAPTER 6

Heartbroken

Our hearts break on so many different levels and times during our journey of motherhood. There are the major heartbreaks—the loss of a child, the failure to conceive—and then things such as helplessly watching our children deal with life's many unpleasant realities. The pain we experience may strike momentarily or may leave its effects for a lifetime. Sorrows should never be drowned; yet there are times when pairing a good wine with the trials of the heart can be very healing.

Dropping My Baby Off at Day Care Broke My Heart

As ironic as it sounds, I had no doubt my heart would be broken on Valentine's Day. You see, my baby girl was born on January 21st, and only three weeks later, I would be standing at the front door of a woman I'd barely even spoken with, ready to hand over my precious newborn to her. It was too soon, but there was no choice.

So the day came, and holding back tears, I stood on the doorstep of the day care for what seemed like an eternity, just staring blankly at the door. It was beige and framed by a pretty, upscale brick house. I guess that should've made me feel better in some weird, only-in-today's-society kind of way. She had a nice house—so surely, she was a good person? That's the way it works, right?

I just stood there staring, holding my sleeping infant close to my chest. I'd dressed her special that day in cute little jeans and a top with hearts on them. Being a new mother, I didn't know the obvious—that jeans are uncomfortable for babies, who actually prefer to be in clothing made of soft fabric. Well, at least she was festively dressed for the holiday on her first day of day care.

Finally, I reached my hand up to knock, but then Callie whimpered so I quickly pulled away. I patted her soft head of dark, messy hair. *Why* was I dropping her off only after three weeks I again asked myself. Oh yes—that's right. *"I have to."*

I'd been working at an insurance agency for about two years and only had three weeks of time to take off. My husband and I were struggling to make ends meet so I had to go back to work. Besides, I was lucky—wasn't I? Most of the other ladies in my office with children had taken only two weeks off.

Bringing me back to reality, Aurea, a beautiful, petite Puerto Rican woman opened the door. I wondered if I'd even knocked. Her eyes filled with confusion as she waved me inside. "Come on in, Trina. How long have you been out here?"

She seemed to sense my fears, or at least understood them from past experience, and gestured for me to sit on her couch. The white carpet looked impeccable, not a spot anywhere. I looked around at the five other young children playing with toys, wondering how on earth she kept her house so perfect. There wasn't a speck of dust anywhere on her expensive furniture. Was this a good sign?

I didn't think so.

We chatted for a few minutes, with mostly me doing the

talking, reminding Aurea of Callie's schedule. Now I laugh at that—schedule? At three weeks? There was no schedule! And the kind gleam in Aurea's eyes said she knew this too.

I hugged my tiny baby girl close to my chest and then turned her over to someone else for the first time. Aurea immediately placed her in a bouncy chair and bustled off into the kitchen, which made me only want to stay longer. She should be held! *All the time!* Trying to stay strong, I forced myself to leave. I drove away, crying—and not just a tear or two, real tears. A veritable deluge was washing down my face. What kind of terrible mother leaves her baby when she's at such a young age? What kind of life was I already setting her up for?

I called to check on Callie about four times that day. Thankfully, Aurea was patient and friendly. Although I was concerned about leaving my daughter, I knew deep down, she was in great hands. I had picked Aurea after having reviewed her huge list of references. Three or four ladies ran a day care in the town where I worked. They worked together and were friends, and all came with great recommendations. But, typically, they all were full, taking no more kids. I still think of Aurea as a huge blessing.

Sometimes, as mothers, we have to do what's best for our children, even if it's tough and tears us apart. Looking back, I believe that Aurea brought something not only to my child, but to my family. She was patient, loving, smart, and incredibly experienced in the area of child rearing and caretaking. By the time Callie was two, she was taking naps at the same time every day. She was cleaning up and putting all her toys back where they belonged. When given a well-balanced lunch, she'd eat it without complaining a lick about it. She was reading books and singing songs I never thought a two-year-old could sing. And she had a heart of gold and a giving nature that I believe could've only partly been born in her and partly taught to her.

DARE TO PAIR

The first day of day care is one of the hardest days of a mother's life for working mommas. There's no getting around it, no avoiding the inevitable heartache. Remember, we're all in this crazy race together—you aren't alone. To help soothe the pain of doing those things you may not want to do, but have to, reward yourself for surviving it with this alternative to traditional reds: **Relax Cool Red**. Typically served chilled, this wine has flavors of black cherries and plums, complemented by soft tannins and a touch of velvety sweetness. After a day like this one, you *deserve* to unwind.

Tears on the First Day of School are Inevitable

Your child's first day of school is one of the most emotionally crazy days you'll ever have. You are conflicted between being excited for them to start a new phase in her life and being sad that the time has passed so quickly that your babies are growing up.

I'll never forget dropping my daughter off for kindergarten at our local elementary school. She had attended both a home day care and a preschool, but this was different. We spent the evening before the big day painting her nails and picking out her outfit, searching for hairstyles on the Internet, and drawing cute letters that spelled out "kindergarten."

Usually, I'm a pretty level-headed woman and not overly emotional. I look forward to each new phase in my kids' lives as a new adventure. So when I woke her up and got her dressed for school that morning, I was confused by all my mixed emotions and silent concerns. Would she eat her lunch or would she be too excited? What if she got lost on her way to class? What if her teacher was too tough or didn't appreciate her loud way of expressing her opinions?

It only got worse as we walked up to the school to get in her class line. An array of students and parents surrounded us; and I found myself studying them. I wondered if the kids were nice. Did they come from good families? Would they be a good influence on my child? My head was buzzing. I looked down at my daughter, though, who was smiling and chipper. I realized she was tugging at me to get us in the line—wanting the day to start.

We said our goodbyes and, as I watched her walk away, she turned to wave and smile—and my first tear rolled down my cheek. While I was excited for her new adventure, I was forlorn that it had come so soon. Then there was a sudden regret that I hadn't spent as much time with her coloring the day before because I had had to cook dinner. I waved back, turned and walked slowly to my car. Once I got in, I stayed there awhile, until the entire parking lot was empty, not ready to leave just yet.

I spent all day wondering how she was doing. Did she miss me? Was she scared in her new school? Would they call me if they needed me? Several times, I stopped myself from calling to check on her because I refused to be one of *those* moms. I was so happy when it was time to pick her up. She came running as soon as she saw me, yelling, "Hi Mommy!" with the biggest smile on her face.

The ride home was filled with tales of how she'd played with her new friends on the playground, eaten in her new lunchroom, how much she enjoyed her teacher, and how excited she was for the next day. I listened intently, with a smile on my face. I realized: *she* was just fine. It was her mother we had to worry about.

Even after my experience with my daughter, when I learned

that our kids are tough—they will be just fine—I did the same thing when I dropped my son off at school. Would he be okay? He wasn't as outgoing as my daughter, what if he needed me? He may not ask for help. And guess what? He not only did well but thrived his first day.

As I get ready to take my third child to her first day of school, I have prepared accordingly—by coloring that extra five minutes before dinner when she asked me to and stocking my car full of tissues.

DARE TO PAIR

No one can truly ready you for the day you'll drop your baby off for their first day of school. It can feel like a punch to your stomach or chin. When the tears start to fall, remember that you are slowly giving them wings, preparing them to fly one day. To help cope, pour yourself some of this velvety smooth **Uppercut Cabernet Sauvignon** by The Wine Bar. Heady with dark fruit and plush textures, it pairs wonderfully with chocolate—and a box of soft tissues.

My Child Has Been Blessed with Two Daddies

I'd called my son's father to discuss the visit to see my son he was planning. After the call, I hung up and said to my son, "Kesel, guess what? Daddy Kris and Tessa and Momma and Daddy Tim and you are *all* going to go out to dinner together!"

He replied, "With you too Momma?"

I told him I would of course be there, noting a bit of relief on his face. These conversations were never easy, as his dad lived so far away and rarely visited. My husband, Tim, had long ago filled the void that his father's absence left in my son's life—so these sudden visits could be challenging. I continued to cook dinner as I kept an eye on Kesel as he played with his toys.

Suddenly he looked up at me. "Mom did you live here when you were a little girl?" motioning around our house as he asked.

"No, I lived in Wyoming by Auntie Morgan's house, remember? I showed you during our last trip."

"Oh yeah." He was quiet for a moment before saying, "Where did daddy live when he was a little boy?"

"Daddy Kris or Daddy Tim?" I had stopped cooking at this point, knowing this conversation was about to get serious.

"Daddy." He said matter-of-factly, deliberately.

"Well you know where Nana Ligon lives? Daddy Tim lived in that house when he was a little boy." I could see him trying to connect the dots.

"Who lived in this house?"

"No one sweetie, we bought this house when we became bigger people."

That seemed to satisfy him so he continued on playing. I sighed in relief, hoping his questions were satisfied. There is nothing harder than being a mom sometimes—we simply *don't* have all the answers.

But as I was tucking him into bed that night, he persisted. "Did I always live here since I was a little boy?"

I gulped, pulling the blanket up around his adorable little face. "No, Kesel, you and Momma and Daddy Kris used to live together in a different house." I replied and picked up the photo of Kris and me with Kesel as a baby, which we kept at his bedside for him. He just stared at the it. I took a breath and continued, "When you were really little, Momma and

Daddy Kris and you all lived together until Daddy Kris had to go a long, long ways to work and then he met Tessa, and Momma met Daddy Tim, and that is how you got two daddies."

My poor little boy looked puzzled, which broke my heart. "I don't understand" he said, as I put the picture down.

"I know buddy, but you don't have to understand right now, just go to sleep and get some rest." I kissed his forehead as I was about to get up to turn off the light.

"But I don't want two daddies."

"Well God has blessed you with two daddies that you get to go and have twice the fun with." I kissed him once again goodnight, watching his frown turn into a small smile.

DARE TO PAIR

Life is never simple, no matter how much you want it to be. It can be heartbreaking to try to explain life's complexities to our children. While the traditional family is important, so, too, can be a blended one. Just as parenthood is a partnership—sometimes with more than one partner—this sweet Trinchero Family Estates' **Mènage à Trois Rosé** is designed as a cocktail of three varieties of blends, as the makers say, "three is better than one." Enjoy its roller coaster of flavors: raspberries, strawberries, lychee nuts, and flowers, all with a silky smooth finish. It will put you in the mood to celebrate the family you have—whatever its form.

This Isn't How I Pictured It at All!

One of the things I dreamed about most when I imagined having children was reading to them in bed, all snuggled beneath the covers, with their heads resting on me. My kids are now two and three, and I'm still waiting for that dream of mine to come true. You see, I have boys.

I started reading to each of them when they were in my belly so reading could become part of our bedtime ritual. It got pretty exciting when Luke began to learn words and we'd slowly browse through a book. I'd point to a picture and he'd holler out the matching word. Then, when he was learning the alphabet, we'd search the pages for letters he recognized.

That turned out to be the extent of our reading.

Two weeks ago, we got him a sturdy, *Cars* toddler bed (within the first hour the *Cars* sticker was ripped off). That night, I climbed into his red bed adorned with *Toy Story* sheets; and he hopped in right next to me. This is it, I thought, anticipating the big moment. he wants me to read to him as he follows the stories along with me. I pulled the sheets up over us, opened the book, and began to read the first page of *Goldilocks and the Three Bears*.

Little brother Zealand—hearing me reading, decided to get in bed, too. How exciting! He climbed up over me, his knees poking my shin, toenails scraping my thigh. But he found a spot, and there we were. Snuggling in closer, I reread the first page so Zealand wouldn't miss a thing.

By page three, as the hungry little blonde comes across the porridge, Luke had turned his body ninety degrees from mine with his feet propped on his bedside table. Apparently he was revving his engine. "Brrrm brrrrm-vroom!" he growled, as a car going really, really fast. Meanwhile Zealand was tugging and bending and shoving the page I was trying to read. His mission was to destroy the page not read it. I swiftly pulled the book from his grip as if I were a three-year-old on the playground, rightfully grabbing back my toy. In response, he pulled himself to his feet and began to bounce up and down. Then,

Luke flipped over and jumped out of bed, elbowing me in my chest, and snatched the book.

"No more book, Mommy!" he announced.

I was heartbroken! My cozy little dream.

Then, without warning, my frustration appeared. I slammed the book shut and said in my stern-mommy voice, "We are going to sit here and read this book, right now, or I am going to leave this room!" That voice is usually saved for moments when he hits his brother or when Zealand tries to scale the entertainment center. I quickly realized it would take more than a new toddler bed, with room for an adult and maybe another child, to sway these boys from their inherent verve.

Defeated, I looked at them, opened my arms out to the room thereby signaling that it was okay for them to run and play, and pulled myself up on the bed. I made a comfy spot and read the familiar story of a broken chair and a little girl fast asleep. In the background, I heard the sound of: my sons making car and helicopter noises; a basketball bouncing off the wall; the click of the fan being turned on and off, then on again; and their loud, boyish laughter.

DARE TO PAIR

When you feel as though your authority as a mother is being rebelled against and are contemplating a mutiny of your own, pour a glass of the luscious **Mutiny**—a Lido Bay vintage blend. This wine is full of flavor with hints of blackberry, cherry, and dark chocolate, along with aromas of lavender, toasted spice, and Tahitian cinnamon—soothing spices that will ease the pangs of your heart.

Sadly, I remembered the many conversations I'd had with friends who had daughters and who could cuddle up with them for book after book after book. I wished that at least one of my boys would want to sit still and read with me. But, watching the joy on their faces as they wildly play with one another right up to the last minutes before bed, I know that I'll happily have to trade-in my dream (for now).

I *Never* Gave Up, Even When I Wanted To

When we welcomed our beautiful son Cody into the world, it had been a perfect storybook pregnancy, the birth had been easy and he was healthy. We were so excited to be parents—life was amazing!

Ready for our little family to grow and for Cody to have a sibling, we were ecstatic two years later when we found out we were pregnant again! Unfortunately, the excitement didn't last long. Two months later, I started bleeding and went to the doctor. Though part of me was scared, another part was not really too concerned—until she told me the devastating news: I was miscarrying.

First, I was shocked, then heartbroken with the news. Then came the most horrible part, waiting for my precious unborn child to pass. It's indescribably painful to carry a baby that you know will never be. You struggle with not wanting to say goodbye but also wanting it to be over with. I held it together on the outside, but I was really very sad and scared. I remember standing in the shower with my hand on my tummy begging God not to take my baby, begging for a miracle.

I did that with *all* of them.

Telling my mom was not easy. She had had her own losses, and I hated bringing her back to that again. She told me I would always be a solitary mourner and that nobody would miss my babies as much as me because no one would feel the kind of connection to them that I did. She was right; but I didn't want it to be that way.

I was later blessed with a wonderful friend, whose story is very similar to mine. She and I have helped each other through some very difficult times. It's so much better when you have someone whom you can just call to say, "It's bad today," and they totally know what you mean and how you feel. She doesn't tell you, "Everything happens for a reason," or "God has a plan," or any of the stuff that people who haven't been there say. She would just tell me, "I know it sucks and you're sad and you ache for your child. I get it, it's okay, and—you're not alone." For some reason, hearing those words consoled me.

A year after the miscarriage, we lost another baby. I was even more devastated this time, if that was possible, and started to worry that something was wrong with me. We found out a week before Thanksgiving. Because I didn't want to ruin the holiday for my family, I didn't tell them and held it together.

Afterwards, I had to get ready for Christmas. While I wanted my young son to have a wonderful holiday, I remember sitting on the couch at my in-laws, watching everyone be so happy, and feeling so detached. I was feeling resentful, but didn't know why exactly. It was like watching a group of happy people through a window and knowing I used to be in there with them but now I'm outside in the cold all by myself, stuck in a world of sadness and disappointment. I was depressed.

We lost baby number three a few years later. I remember what my husband, Jason, was wearing that day. Even though I'd been through it before, I remember every feeling and every thought. I can still see myself sitting in the waiting room, knowing what the doctors were going say and trying not to cry. The same day that we got the news that our baby had passed away, my beautiful nephew was born. A few weeks later when my brother-in-law's car came up the driveway, I ran away to a back bedroom, crying. I couldn't face meeting my nephew for the first time. And when Jason brought him in to me, I held him close and cried, aching to hold my own lost baby, a baby that would never be. It was one of the hardest and most vivid moments in my life; and one that still brings tears to my eyes.

Baby number four came and went about two years later. By that point, I was not only sad but pretty angry, and, to be honest—I'd pretty much given up. I was even more depressed, but had hardened as a person. Over the year that followed, I had come to the realization that I would have to accept that we'd only have one child. I knew he was a huge blessing and was so thankful we had him. It was just that, I'm an only child, I wanted Cody to have a sibling so much. I tried to come to terms with the fact he'd never have a sister or a brother and eventually started to let it go, although there would always be the ache for another child deep under the surface.

A few more years passed by. I'd been barely paying attention—then I realized I was *late*! It turned out I was pregnant, yet again. This time we wanted to keep the news to ourselves. It was stressful, but we couldn't help but be cautiously optimistic. The weeks went on—no issues, no bleeding. Waiting made me a total wreck waiting! Finally, 15 weeks later (longest weeks of my life) the docs said I was most likely in the clear. I was overjoyed! God had heard my prayers, he had been listening all along. One of the most amazing things was telling Cody that, finally, after all those years, he was going be a big brother! We didn't want to know if it was boy or girl because we didn't care. Even, when my son Cade was born, I didn't bother to check. I just reached out to grab him and hold him tight.

My world became right again. It was as if the clouds had lifted and the sun was finally shining on my world. Cade filled a huge hole in my heart and everyone else's as well. Friends seemed to notice a difference in me, telling me how good and happy I looked. Some of my newer friends had *never* seen me like that—it was a revelation for them.

Life was good! Cody loved and still loves being a big brother. Soon, Cade will be a big brother too! Yes, another boy is coming. While I'll always miss all my babies and never understand the reason I lost them, I thank God every day for our growing family and I don't focus on the past anymore. Life is too precious and short to be anything but thankful for the future.

DARE TO PAIR

There are many moms whose personal heartaches make them feel like a prisoner within their own walls. Before succumbing to those stifling, cold-metal bars forever, remember that blessings come often and in many forms—we just can't give up. Even if it doesn't feel like a jolly good time, treat yourself to a glass of wine, at least, for its relaxing effect on your psyche. You deserve a break. We recommend this blend of Zinfandel, Cabernet Sauvignon, Syrah, Petite Sirah and Grenache from The Prisoner Wine Company called **The Prisoner**. Featuring enticing aromas of bing cherry, espresso, and roasted fig and flavors of ripe raspberry, pomegranate, and wild berry.

Talking to My Child about a Death in the Family

I'll never forget that evening. After getting home late from an event with friends, my ex-husband called me to say "Grandma died tonight."

Our precious Grandma from Oklahoma flashed in my mind: A big woman, who loved to have her hair done and wear colorful floor-length, silk nightgowns. We adored her deep-fried spreads—that woman could make chicken-fried deer steak like it was nobody's business. Every time we were going to visit, I prayed that she'd make chicken fingers or Indian Tacos or another one of her specialties.

When we had our first child, Callie, we lived in Oklahoma near all the family. Grandma loved her at first sight and wanted her with her all the time. As Callie grew older, we'd have to fight Grandma tooth and nail for sneaking our daughter ice cream or candy too much. Whatever Callie wanted, Grandma got her. When Callie turned two, we moved to Colorado. The entire family was devastated, but nothing like Grandma. She cried for weeks and tried to talk us out of moving. I promised to send her lots of pictures and that we'd visit when we could.

Because of her health issues, in our hearts, we knew we needed to visit often. You never know how long you have someone. We made a couple trips a year, usually during the summer and at Thanksgiving. I can still feel the warm Oklahoma mornings and the smell of Grandma's breakfast wafting through the house as we were getting up.

Callie loved these visits, and, as she grew older, she'd talk to Grandma on the phone more and more frequently. Grandma, it seemed, often knew more about what was going on with Callie than we did. The special bond they'd formed was like no other. I'll admit I probably didn't value it enough—until she was gone.

I sat down on my bed after the phone call and cried because I knew we'd have to tell our baby girl that her precious Grandma had passed. And I cried because she'd e-mailed me just the week before telling me that, despite her grandson's and my divorce, she loved me and that I was a great mom. Finally, I cried because I never got to tell her, despite all the things she'd done for me, how much I appreciated her. But, mostly, I cried for my baby girl, not knowing how she'd take the news.

The next day, my ex-husband was going to bring my kids to the funeral. I felt horrible because he was the one who was going to tell them about Grandma's passing. I'd always been the rock that held everything together so it was hard for me to let them deal with this one on their own. Once he'd told Callie, he called and reported, "She took it surprisingly well."

"What did she say?" I wanted details. What I really wanted was to have been there, to help her.

"She cried for a second, but she seemed to understand she's in heaven."

My six-year-old girl took the news like a grown-up. At the funeral, she had only shed a few tears. And she brought home with her some of Grandma's precious jewelry and nightgowns, which she still wears to this day.

The other day, we were driving down the road. I looked at the rearview mirror and saw that Callie was crying in the backseat. When I asked her what was wrong, she replied, "I miss Grandma Betty," wiping a tear from her face. My precious child. So smart, and so adult-like. She'd been holding in the pain.

"Sweetie, Grandma is looking down on you from Heaven. She can see you now, and you can pray to her every night if you'd like." That seemed to calm her; and that very night, as I walked past her room after she'd gone to bed, I heard: "Dear Grandma up in Heaven. I miss you so much. My mommy wouldn't give me any candy tonight again. She said you could see me. Can you see me? I miss you very much and I wish you could come home."

In the wake of a loved one's death, I've learned that it may seem as though our children are more resilient than we could ever imagine. However, they may be fighting a silent battle with grief that we must become aware of and support. While Grandma may be gone, she will live forever in my little girl's heart.

DARE TO PAIR

We may never feel truly up to the task of navigating the landmine that is explaining death to our children. What makes it harder is that, often, we are also having our own feelings about it. If you need a small bit of help amping up your courage or simply want to say a toast to the departed, try this medium-bodied, buttery **Seven Heavenly Chardonnay** (Michael and David Winery), with currants and a hint of peach jam. Just as intense as explaining to your babies that their Grandma is in heaven, this wine could be your saving grace.

We Planned and Planned, but God Had a Different Plan

After losing my first child, Jordan, to SIDS, my husband and I quickly had another baby, a boy. I felt so blessed to be able to focus on a new baby rather than on the devastating loss of Jordan. It was just a happy occasion after such a tragedy. Then, 18 months later, we had another boy.

Of course, I was so excited to have him and wouldn't change a thing now, but, secretly, I'd been hoping to have another little girl. I wasn't looking to replace Jordan by any means—we still celebrate her birthday every year—but when we got pregnant again I couldn't wait to find out what it was and bought the DNA finger-prick test. When the test came back, it was a girl! I was *so* excited and ready to welcome our little princess into the world that even the baby shower invites were pink. When I had my ultrasound, the doctor said he couldn't tell what it was. (Today I'm pretty sure that he just didn't tell me the truth because he knew I wanted a girl so badly). But as it turned out, we had another baby boy. Lesson learned: don't buy the DNA tests and save your $200.

Four years flew by as we were busily raising our three boys, whom we loved to pieces. We were not planning on having another baby, but I wasn't exactly great at taking my pills every day, so there I was—pregnant again.

This time, I decided I didn't want to find out what the sex of the baby was. I was going to be excited either way and reined in my expectations. At the ultrasound, I told my doctor not to tell me, "By the fifth baby, it doesn't matter what it is." Deep down, however, I can admit now that I again hoped for a little princess.

Immediately regretting my decision, as soon as I left the hospital, I felt immense anxiety because that had been the only ultrasound I was going to have. Still, as time went on, I couldn't help but notice how tired I was and that brushing my teeth made me gag, which were the same symptoms I had had almost 10 years earlier with my first baby girl. But, not wanting to get my hopes up, I pushed those thoughts aside.

Soon enough I found myself at the hospital with the doc saying, "Well I think we're going to do this." I was admitted and moved into a birthing room. Because it seemed to be the *same* room where I had had Jordan, I had the fleeting thought that this baby *had* to be a girl, but I quickly let it go because you *never* really know.

I waited and waited, but nothing was happening. Other

women came to deliver and were in full-on labor. The doctors and nurses delivered three boys ahead of me. This made me decide that I was definitely going to have another boy. Once things started to move, and a rough (for me) labor, there was my baby—a precious little pink being that I desperately wanted to hold. My doctor looked at my husband and said, "Did you see what it is?"

Now both of them were grinning.

"What is it?" I asked desperately.

Everyone responded: "It's a girl."

So, after the tragedy, our three beautiful boys, and one unplanned pregnancy, our little girl arrived to complete our family of, now, six—and my heart was full. I will never stop missing our eldest child, Jordan, but she will forever be part of our family and in our hearts, just as God intended.

DARE TO PAIR

Life is about creating and celebrating your own story, even if it didn't go exactly as planned. But everyone's fairy tale is just a little different. Toast your own "once upon a time" story with this cool yet crisp and refreshing **Once Upon a Vine Lost Slipper Sauvignon Blanc**, by The Wine Bar, with flavors of citrus and lemon chiffon. While it all depends on how you look at it, technically, we *all* live happily ever after.

CHAPTER 7

Annoyed by Grownups

Motherhood is challenging, but sometimes it can actually seem like a piece of cake compared to the complexities of our relationships with other grownups. From other moms to our husbands—or even complete strangers—adults can be irritating if not completely maddening.

Pour a glass of the lovely pairings we've suggested below and revel in the fact that being mommy dearest to your children isn't the hardest relationship of them all.

What's *Your* Superpower?

"I know you're nervous about telling people, but here's my one piece of advice—don't let anyone steal your joy." Those were the words of a good friend, a mother of two children only a year apart in age. I tried to truly let them sink in. She gave me this advice right after I told her I was pregnant—again—for the fourth time. "Who cares what they think anyway?! Have they seen your kids?! They're *beautiful*," she went on.

I had to stop and think about *why* I cared what anyone thought. Maybe it was because it seems to be a societal norm that you are only supposed to have two gender-opposite children ranging around two to five years apart. If you are "unlucky" enough to get two children of the same gender, you may try for a third strike, but, beyond three, nowadays you are considered a *large* family. This is also apparently equivalent to a tragic event and completely freaky.

I have three daughters, ages five, three, and eighteen months. I'll have my fourth child when my youngest will be not quite two-years-old. (Note: I do not know the gender of our fourth child nor do I want to know. I want to be surprised—and that's a whole other public debate.)

Maybe my trepidation stems from the fact that people have not always been that receptive to me when I told them that I was expecting. My oldest was conceived right at the same time my husband and I got engaged. My second daughter may have come at a time when people didn't think we were financially stable enough, and—gasp—our *third* daughter couldn't have been *planned*, right?!

And *now*, holy bananas, hold on to your hats folks, we are having a *fourth* child. We *must* be insane for wanting all these kids. Even the nurse at the obstetrician's office jokingly said, "Wait, all three of those girls are *yours*? Don't you know where babies come from?"

I decided not to make a big announcement about my latest until I hit the halfway mark, giving myself plenty of time to be ready to deal with the comments, the questions, and the stares. But, I simply couldn't hide the baby bump anymore (there are only so many extra-large T-shirts I want to wear) so on Mother's Day I announced to the world (via Facebook and Instagram) that we were going to be a family of six. I braced myself for the comments. Many were positive, but what I didn't know was that, behind the scenes, certain people felt the need to ask my friends about it.

"Do you know how many people have asked me if this baby

of yours was planned?" my best friend wondered. I looked at her wide-eyed.

"What!" I demanded, "Who the hell thinks they have any right to know the details of decisions made in my bedroom between myself, my husband and God?!" I was floored.

"Lots of people, apparently," she simply said, as she walked on and drank her Starbucks.

Whoa. I thought. Really? People want to know if this was planned?! I silently screamed obscenities at these individuals who weren't brave enough to ask *me* about my family planning. Why are people so obsessed with knowing whether a pregnancy was planned or unplanned?

Dear people, who are so curious, all babies are planned, divinely chosen by God in the preexistence, to be put on earth to live a life of purpose. I'm just grateful to have been chosen as a mother and given the responsibility of raising children and loving them as much as I possibly can. That's my job.

Usually, when people are nosy about a pregnancy in this way, they also, in that same breath, ask how many children we *want.* Um, all of them? Is that an acceptable answer? Or, how about this one: "Why don't we have a sit-down and talk about family planning and you can tell me how many children you think I should plan on having? Does next week look good for you to have this oh-so-comfortable conversation that you're interested in?"

Sometimes I will answer the flat truth: "My husband wanted two. We are now having our fourth. Yes, we wanted all of these children. They are wonderful blessings who fill our lives with joy."

I'm not quite sure when we as a society decided that we should make judgments about what happens between spouses and God—especially about family size. Have just one child, and you are obviously spoiling them beyond measure and are too selfish to give them a sibling. Do you have a boy and a girl? If yes, then you are obviously the perfect family; why would you want to change that? But if you have two of the same gender, then, clearly, you are going to try for one of the opposite gender. Have four or more, and people think you belong in the circus. Or want your own reality show.

Because that's my plan for retirement: a TV show about my oldest daughter singing the soundtrack to *Frozen* every day: my middle daughter cracking jokes: and my youngest, who is still not talking, screaming at me for not holding her all the time. And a camera following me around without my makeup and still in my yoga pants at 10 a.m. Yep, that's *exactly* what I have in mind. Honestly. As a society, we should start keeping our noses in our own business and supporting other parents in this crazy journey that is parenthood.

I hope I can raise my kids with the decency to tell people "congratulations!" when they are sharing good news. Because *that*, folks, is the appropriate answer. Any woman brave enough to tell you she's pregnant usually has a lot more going on than just that. As excited as she is, she's probably also terrified, terrified of what's happening to her body, of what becoming a mother means. (Whether it's her first or her fifth, she's questioning her abilities to raise a human being.) There are a lot of things she's scared about, but what she shouldn't be scared of is people's reactions.

To all you women who are afraid of what society will say to you when you finally get to use that super-cute Pinterest pregnancy-announcement idea, remember this mantra: "I grow humans, what's *your* super-power?" Embrace motherhood; embrace what your life is going to become when you decide to have a family. Enjoy the ride. It doesn't last nearly long enough. Of course, then you can just have another and ride it all over again. Or not—I won't judge.

DARE TO PAIR

People can be nosy, opinionated, and downright rude. About the time you want to become a complete bitch and sass those jerks right back, take a gulp or two of this distinctly sweet **Sassy Bitch Moscato**. Containing orange, mango, honey, and vanilla flavors—this vino will remind you that your life is your life and your joy may not be the joy of others.

Finding Friends as a Mom Is Nearly as Difficult as Parenting Itself

Have you ever noticed how trying to meet other moms is kind of similar to trying to pick someone up back in our singleton days? I first realized this when I moved to a new town with two young boys. I wanted someone to spend my mom time with at all those endless parks and playgrounds. Hopefully someone who could make me laugh. Someone I could chat with about mothering, movies (*as if* I actually have time for those these days), favorite restaurants, dieting, reality TV and, *of course*, Oprah's Lifeclass.

After about six weeks of living here in sunny Florida, I discovered the area's one-and-*only* Chick-fil-A. My hopes for a new friend soared. This place is a mom magnet!

This particular day was not unlike most days I've spent there over the last few months. I spot her first. Or I think I do. She's cute. Stylish! She has as many, if not more, kids than me, so I know she'll *get* me. We smile at one another. Finally, one of us has enough nerve to speak up.

"How old is your little cutie?"

"Three-and-a-half. How about your little girl? How old is that precious doll?" *See, we're both trying to impress with flattery!*

"Just turned four." *Cool. We've got kiddos close to the same age.*

"Do you live here?" *We live in a very touristy town—so this is a mandatory question!*

"Yes, we moved here a couple of years ago. We're Air Force. You?"

"We just moved here a couple of months ago. We're really enjoying it. Great for the kids!"

"Yeah, it sure is."

Quiet.

That uncomfortable silence. We both pick up our phones. I'm checking my e-mail, trying desperately to be cool. I glance up, she's looking at me. *She's interested!*

"Where did you move here from?" She asks. *Woot! She wants to talk!*

"Charleston, South Carolina." I smile.

"Oh, it's beautiful there!"

"Yes, it is! We loved it there! But it's gorgeous here!"

And during the next thirty minutes we talk about our kids and schools and friends and church and other playgrounds in the area.

"Emma Jane, five more minutes and we have to go pick up your sister." She hollers towards the slide. That's when the panic sets in. *Do I ask for her number? Will she ask for mine? We both have cell phones, we could easily type them in. No pens or paper needed. What if I never see her again!*

We chat a few minutes more.

"Emma Jane, put on your shoes please. It's time to go." I decide I'm not going to ask for her number. It might seem desperate.

"Thank you so much for all the tips you've given me about this area. I can't wait to start checking out preschools!" I say, a little too peppy.

"Absolutely! We're here every week, usually Mondays or Thursdays. I'm sure we'll see you again! It was nice to meet you!"

Emma Jane's mommy warmly says good-bye, then, "My name is Jenny."

"I'm Leah. Nice talking to you." They leave.

I feel good about this one. She was sincere, sweet. Who's got time for numbers anyway with raising kiddos! I pack up my boys and we head out to our car. My son asks, "When are we going to see Emma Jane again?"

"Soon, baby, soon." And I say this with great faith. Meeting new friends may not be easy for a mom in a new town, but I have a good feeling about today.

DARE TO PAIR

The pale yellow and green hues of this fruity **Nice to Meet You, Adegas Castrobrey** will remind you of the park where you spent the afternoon trying to make that new friend. It will leave you with both a citric aftertaste and the optimism that new friendships are just around the corner.

Challenging Parents

My blood raced through my veins as my heart beat rapidly in my chest. Was I reading this e-mail right? She's taking her son out of my son's class—literally requesting a room change—

because my son said to her son, "I don't want to play with you."

My mind searched back on memories of happy playdates, festive parties, and two best buddies playing on the soccer field together. In almost a year of our sons' friendship, we had never had any drama or issues, not to mention any altercations. I think the worst scolding we'd ever had to give them was, "You boys have to share!"

So there we were, just a few days after our last friendly play-date, when she and I had talked about kids and husbands and life before Florida. Not a word had been said about any negative feelings between my son and hers. Now, three days later, I'm reading an e-mail describing her son's discomfort around my son for the past few weeks. A few weeks! Why couldn't she have said something at the playdate? Or when they were at my house last week? Or when we were at soccer? How about when I passed her thirty minutes ago in the preschool hallway? All that happened then was just a smile and a hello—no heads up to prepare me for this e-mail that made no sense to me. Passive-aggressive much?

Rather than write her in a frenzied, highly-emotional response, I knew I needed to talk it over with my husband. "What'd she say, exactly?" he asked when I burst into tears and rambled on about the e-mail.

"She said that she was taking Paul out of Logan's class because Logan said he didn't want to play with Paul and something about last week Logan stomped Paul on the foot after Paul took a jeep from Logan. But, you know Logan, he never hits or kicks anyone. The teachers never told me about this. This is crazy!" I explained.

"She even said that her son has been coming home crying every day because Logan is playing with other kids. They're four! What does she want? And this makes her want to change classes? Who would do that to their kid? I mean, yeah, if there was a bully in the class, *maybe*. But, because of these things—it's extreme! It will only confuse her child if he has to switch classes right now, one month before school gets out."

Ridiculousness.

My husband hugged me. "Don't worry about her. She's being immature and needs to grow up a bit. What do they call it? 'a helicopter mom,' trying to control every little issue in her child's life."

This calmed me a bit. Of course, that's it! She's *that* type of mom. I'm not. I'm all about letting children deal with adversity and work things out for themselves. How else will they learn to be functioning adults? After speaking to my husband, I felt better. I went home and wrote in response, "I'm sorry you feel that way. I wish Paul the best of luck in his new class." Simple.

However, I called the school and set up a conference with Logan's teacher. I needed to get to the bottom of this for my own conscience. I knew in my heart that Logan was a good kid. We'd never had issues of him fighting with other children. In fact, many parents we'd meet would praise us for how we've raised our boys so far. One mom even asked if she could enroll her kids in my "child boot camp" so they would behave as well as mine. No, my child isn't perfect, but he's not the type of who would make you want to move your child to another class.

After meeting with the teachers and hearing that Logan is an exceptional student who shows more kindness than most at his age; I went home feeling on top of the world. They even told me that he showed great maturity in "using his words," rather than pushing or hitting.

It was then I knew this was just the *beginning* of dealing with other parents, who handle things differently than my husband and I do and often in a way we won't understand or even agree with. This experience hurt because it involved a friend, but it paved the tumultuous road for future interactions with the variety of parents that I'd be meeting along this road of parenthood.

DARE TO PAIR

Oh, they're out there—and they always will be—*other parents*. Some of them will seem unfathomable to you. They'll make decisions that make your head spin. Just stay calm and stay out of judgment. But do not fret sister friend, there's always the refined **The Sophisticate Zinfandel**, from Four Vines Winery. The myriad flavor notes in this one—a nose of licorice, smoked meat, and blackberries, the intriguing oak notes of cinnamon and butterscotch, and flavors of boysenberry with a hint of vanilla—will completely divert your attention away from those pesky other parents.

Daddy Always Gets to Be the Fun Parent

Will daddies always go down in history as being the fun ones? *Daddy* catches frogs, wrestles, and throws the kids high in the air, followed by a big splash down in the ocean. *Daddy* serves milkshakes to go with the yummy burgers he grills. *Daddy* lets them watch crazy things on TV that mommy would never allow them to. Daddy plays games, draws them whatever they request, and rides down the tallest waterslide with them wrapped in his strong arms. Daddy's the one who tickles them to alertness right as their sleepy eyes start to droop, ready for to sleep, in front of the movie we're watching—right before bedtime.

Daddy's so fun! So, what does that make me, *Mommy*? The rule maker. The meal server. The snack distributer. The chauffeur, the maid, the one who is always telling them to "pick that up, don't climb so high, be nice to your brother, slow down, brush your teeth, it's time for bed."

I want to be fun, too! But I have too much responsibility. Not to mention the fact that they're with me all day long. When daddy walks through the door after a long, hard day at work, he's something fresh and exciting. He picks them up and throws them in the air with a smile. Pure glee!

It's at that moment, seeing the huge grins on their faces that it occurs to me: we are *both* there for them. They adore us both. While we both play different roles, the end result is that they feel cared for, protected, and happy.

DARE TO PAIR

When daddy seems to be the king of all that is good and amusing in your home, have a little fun of your own and escape with an elegant glass of **Downton Abbey Bordeaux Claret** (Dulong Grand Vins). A glass of this dry, red wine reveals gorgeous scents of wild berries including blackberries, raspberries, and black currants. On the palate, ripe-fruit flavors merge seamlessly with velvety tannins, so this wine is sure to help sweeten the bitter taste in your mouth on the days when you feel like you always come in second.

Even though I may miss out on being the *fun one* most of the time, what I provide is just as important, if not more, in their tiny lives. The structure and nurturing that I give them helps them feel secure; and the fun they have with daddy makes them happy. And though you may not see it today, what I'm doing is building the stepping stones to what I hope will be a successful future for them. So it brings me solace to know that, while Daddy really is very important, mommy is *too*.

I Refuse to Apologize If My Children Are Viewed as a Nuisance

"*Thank you* for bringing your children to the pool," she said dryly.

Yep, that's what the grumpy, frumpy woman who was sunbathing across the pool from us said. I had had my eye on her since my sons and I had arrived thirty minutes earlier along with my friend and her two sons—a total of four young boys between the ages of four and seven. Take that, you peace seekers! As if I'm bringing my children to the pool solely to ruin your peace and quiet. . . .

When we got to the pool, there were no other families there, no children, just three older couples. We opened the gate and all four boys excitedly ran through and jumped right into the crystal-clear pool. Once up for air, they immediately began to clap wild splashes against the water, whooping and hollering. My friend and I laid out towels, set out snacks, and sat down in the warm sun. Not much makes me happier than to watch my sons frolic in the fresh air, especially at the pool or the beach.

Often, there are young women there all dozing peacefully in their lounge chairs, reading magazines, sipping soft drinks—I remember *those* days. Alas, things change. Though I want to respect people's right to relaxation, I can't limit my sons' freedom or love of fun in the sun. After all, this *is* a family pool.

So there we were, my friend and I catching up on one another's lives. Our boys playing as boys would in the pool.

Every so often, one would get out of the pool only to run and jump back in. A few cannonballs were announced, obviously. Two of the couples there smiled and watched the kids having their fun. I did have to call out a couple of times to my sons, "No running! That's how we fall. Walk, please!" But, other than that, they were just boys playing in the pool.

In the thirty minutes we were there, the lady who grumbled at us when we came in moved her chair three times in a huff, even though none of her locations were close to our boys. But our pool is not huge, and the boys' laughter could still be heard all around it.

The children continued to play, exiting the pool every so often for string cheese or grapes or a sip of water. My friend and I continued to watch our kiddos and chat. Then I noticed the unhappy-with-life lady frantically grab her belongings and make her way towards the exit, which was just past where I sat. I tried to ignore her because, frankly, it aggravates me when people are annoyed by my kids when they're simply being kids, especially when we're somewhere that's supposedly "family friendly." I really didn't think she'd say anything. Then she *did*.

"*Thank you* for bringing your children to the pool and letting them take over."

A response to this required quick wit, which was more than my sun-relaxed mind could manage at that moment. Instead I replied, "You're welcome. We'll be here all week!" with a beaming smile and a look right into her eyes. She was walking away when I called out, "Just so you know, it's a family pool!"

More affected than I thought I'd be by the episode, I felt irritated that she'd had the nerve to actually say something to me, putting negativity into my day. It make me angry that there are always people who are annoyed by children, yet, at the same time, I always end up feeling guilty for some reason about it. Kids will always just be kids so why does it bother me?

My friend and I spent the next several minutes talking about how we should have handled the situation. Ultimately, we decided, no matter where you are, there will be cranky, unpleasant people. It doesn't pay to let them disturb you and affect your kids in any way. If she truly wanted the pool all to herself without having to deal with children, then she should consider adults-only pool next time—in another country! In the meantime, we'll continue to enjoy our summer—and let our kids be kids.

DARE TO PAIR

This summer, when your kids are living life to the fullest, join in on the fun with a glass of **Woop Woop Shiraz**. This deep-hued wine bursts with flavors reminiscent of childhood including blueberry jam and licorice. Drink in this full-bodied and flavorsome red and don't give a hoot what other people think.

My Husband Resents Me Having a Girls' Night Out. *Seriously?*

It's finally Girls' Night Out—your monthly outing with mommy friends. You've been waiting 29 days for this, and your husband has known about it for at least the last two weeks of that time. You even had the courtesy to remind him two days ago. Now here you are—on the eve of freedom, at least two to three hours' worth—and your baby's daddy has the nerve to pout and sarcastically remark sideways to the kids, "Mom is going out tonight. Guess we're on our own. Daddy's babysitting again."

Seriously??

Or maybe he said, "You don't see *me* going out with my friends."

Or better yet: "Why do you need to go out anyway?"

Wait. *What?*

Babysit? You think what you're doing is being the babysitter when I ask you one night a month to stay home and watch our kids? Isn't this your duty and pleasure in being Dad? You have got to be kidding me right now!

In fact, no, I don't see you go out with your friends. But, you should. By golly, you probably need to get out and have fun as much as I do. Well, maybe not as much because you have work as a social outlet. Yes, I mean that. You my darling, already get a break.

And why *exactly* do I need to go out? Because it will make me a better mom, a better wife too! It makes me feel refreshed and relaxed. It's a break from the family, getting me out of the house and far, far away from laundry and dishes. It takes place in a happy place where dinner is made for me and then dirty dishes are whisked out of my sight before I even have time to notice.

Seeing my friends means that I can laugh my cares away, cares that we all share. Plus there's no one crying for Mommy, no one needing tending to. It's just me, my glass of wine, and some great conversation with other moms, who all go through the exact same things as me. Can you *blame* me?

Invariably, a "moms' night out" starts with a rant by one of my friends about how her husband planted a guilt trip on her before she left the house so that she's downing her first glass of wine in record time just to soothe her frustration. "Obviously, my husband wants me to have that extra drink tonight!" she laughs as she raises her hand to order another glass.

Once we compare notes, it's nearly always the same story: our husbands laid on the guilt in one form or another when we were about to leave for the night out that we so desperately needed. Note: There is a story floating around about how one mom's husband actually encourages her to go out because he realizes it makes her happy and therefore ultimately happier at home. So if this guy isn't some mythical creature like the unicorn, it seems that some understanding husbands do exist. But they are few and far between.

Some husbands *purposely* come home from work late, leaving mom to race out the door only to have her evening cut short since she's joining the group later than she had hoped. Others have to make the snarky remarks. Or some simply just sulk.

Moms not only need a break, they deserve one. Our hubbies need to quit making us feel like crap for it. So, rather than let him have it for not considering *my* needs on these occasions, I've tried a new approach: communication. I let him know how much I appreciate the nights he doesn't get sarcastic with me about having time out with the girls, whether he's joking or *not*. I thank him, telling him how much I appreciate that he understands something so simple, but which makes me a better mom in the long run. And as much as I have to nearly choke before saying it, I tell him I appreciate the fact he works so hard for our family and wants to be an equal playing partner in this game we call life and parenting.

I think communication wins half the battle. Expressing my gratitude wins the other half—wink, wink!

DARE TO PAIR

If the father of your children is giving you a hard time because he has to do his duty and pitch in as a dad by "gifting" you with a much-deserved night out with friends—quiet his voice by pouring yourself a full-bodied **Tait Barossa Valley The Ball Buster**. This wine is a deep purple, nearly black, and laced with intense aromas of stewed plums, cherry, and chocolate. After a glass or two of this red blend—with or without your man's approval—your night is already off to a great start!

Apparently, *Daddy* Didn't Do It That Way As a Kid

"When I was a kid," (there he goes again) "we didn't have to wear bike helmets and look how we turned out. We turned out just *fine*." I turned away as I rolled my eyes. *Seriously?*

"When I was a kid, we rode in the back of the station wagon without seat belts so we could look out the back window. We were *fine*."

Oh, and then there is: "When I was a kid, we used to play outside for hours and come home with a million bug bites. No one used bug spray, and we *survived*." Ya, our moms probably had some plant or natural thing that repelled bugs, I thought to myself.

"So our kids *have to* drink out of fancy water bottles or cups with built-in straws? Back in my day, we just drank water straight from the hose!" Oy vey.

"What are you doing to that kid? He looks like Casper the Friendly Ghost. When I was young, we hardly ever wore sunscreen and sometimes came home with a little burn. So what? It makes you *tough*."

These opinions might sound farfetched to you in this day and age, but—that's my husband. And, yes, I have to live with him.

If I have to hear my husband say, "When I was a kid . . ." one more time, I might just scream. Sure, I think, you turned out all right (debatable), but you're oblivious to the statistics and news reports about children who didn't turn out fine doing things the old way, *your way.*

The old ways aren't necessarily any better than today. I mean, are we going to deprive our children of baths in the bathtub because in the olden days they used to have to heat the water manually?

So I tell him *once more* that all those *silly* precautions he pokes fun at exist for a reason today and we are going to keep them. Then I keep slathering on the sunscreen, spraying on the bug spray, and clipping on the helmets.

DARE TO PAIR

Times have changed and your children are growing up in a brave new world. When you are getting too much new advice from others, it's time to grab a bottle of **Old Fart Syrah/Grenache**. Delicate, fruity, and spicy, with blackberry flavors and a touch of licorice, this robust and spicy Rhone red will help you easily drown out the unwelcome advice that comes your way.

Making Couple Friends

A few months ago, I met a mom whose son went to preschool with my son. When my little boy came home talking about all the fun he had with her little boy, I tracked her down in the parking lot of our school one afternoon and gave her my number. "Hi, I'm Jennifer, Matthew's mom. Matthew is always talking about your son so I thought we should maybe set up a playdate." She smiled. A great sign! And she looked like she might be pretty cool too, so I was happy. After several playdates with our four boys playing super well together, we made it official by friending one another on Facebook. We had a ton in common, and hanging out with her was always a good time.

After a few more fun playdates, we were ready to take our relationship to the next level. She suggested, "You guys should come over for dinner sometime. I think our husbands would get along, don't you?"

And, I did. The thing is: my husband is usually happiest when he's *not* socializing. He's got his core friends and likes to be at home when he's not busy working. I'm the one in our relationship who enjoys being social, making new friends, and actually hanging out with them. So he needed a bit of encouragement.

And the truth was, I'd only met her husband a few times so I couldn't say for sure whether they would hit it off. Anyway, I enjoyed her so much and how well our kids got along that I tried to be confident. We hammered down a date and set out to introduce our husbands.

As I waited for the dinner date to come, I felt a bit nervous over what would happen. It's hard enough trying to make new friends once you're a mom because not only do you and the other mom have to like each other, but your kids have to get along as well. That's tough enough, then, if you're like me and want relationships where whole families get together for backyard barbecues and football games, the men have to get along too.

As it turned out, the dinner was fantastic! The two men did get along really well, the kids happily hung out together, and, as always, she and I laughed. Success!!

Once we got home I texted her a big thank-you for inviting us over, suggesting they come to our place in a couple of weeks once we'd come back from vacation. She texted me back that she was glad we had finally gotten the guys together. Then she wrote, "How does he feel about my husband? It's like we are setting up a couple! LOL!" And it was funny because it was so true!

I told her I thought our husbands were a perfect match and that I think we'll have a very happy future together—all eight of us.

DARE TO PAIR

Meeting and making new friends is not easy. When you do succeed, toast friendship with this **Hook & Ladder Late Harvest Gewurztraminer**. This wine features the rich flavors and vibrant aromas of the tropical fruits–orange, lemon, grapefruit, peach and apricot– paired with notes of honey and a spicy finish. After a couple of glasses with your new friends, you will feel the bond of your new friendship grow.

CHAPTER 8

Enlightened

As humans, we're always learning. As moms, we tend to forget this; that every day in large and small ways we *are* learning lessons—how to be a better mom, how to approach our children's unique personalities, how to let go of our preconceived notions. Typically, it's our *own* mistakes that teach us the most.

Take time each evening to recap your day; and you'll notice how much you can challenge yourself by revising your expectations, and adjusting your approach. Enjoy some quiet reflection as you unwind with a glass of wine and be enlightened to all that's new and more importantly . . . all that you're actually *already* doing right.

I Thought I Was a Perfect Mom—Until I Had Kids

Bless her heart. It sounds so sweet, doesn't it?

"Bless her heart; I hope she feels better soon." That's so sweet!

"Bless her heart, I know she's worked so hard to get her degree and look how happy she is now!" Awww!

I've been living in the South now for nearly thirteen years now and I've learned that "bless her heart" isn't always as *precious* as it sounds. I've overheard a conversation or two that sounded like this: "Bless her heart, that shirt just makes her look 10 pounds heavier . . . doesn't she realize that?" Or "Bless her heart; she's been a hot *mess* since her husband left her!" But, I've also heard it used when people genuinely think others are endearing or, sometimes, even naive, like when moms with more experience hear new moms expound on their parenting philosophy.

I came across a blog yesterday titled "Things That First Time Moms Say That Been-There-Done-That Moms Laugh At" and as I read it, I could just hear the words "bless her heart" echoing in some of the comments. At first, the title seems malicious ("laugh at"), but if you're a veteran mom, you'll remember you were once a new mom with some pretty crazy ideas too. And I'm not sure wiser moms laugh at new moms per se—maybe just chuckle as we remember our own naiveté. We all learn through our own experiences.

The last of my friends to have a baby, I remember how they'd get a certain look in their eye when I'd talked about how you could get potty training right on the first try because there was the *best* book about it or how, when *my* children grew to be toddlers, they'd behave at restaurants because all my husband and I would have to do is give them *the* look. Now, I know exactly what their eyes were saying to me: just wait.

We've all thought or said some things before we knew better. I remember being pregnant watching a mom feed her toddler french fries at a Chick-fil-A and saying to a friend, "I won't let my children *touch* fast food until they're at least in middle school. You've got to feed them right!" Later I found myself doing the drive-thru thing after missing lunchtime because of a doctor's appointment. I had two hungry, fussy toddlers and a 30-minute drive home.

You live and you learn. Sometimes you go up the learning curve slower than other moms, and sometimes you pick up on things quicker than some. What I have learned is that I'm not perfect, so I shouldn't judge other moms for not being perfect either or for not realizing something until they're ready and have *been there* themselves. We all learn, grow, and become who we are as mothers at our own pace. We should always understand and support that process in ourselves, and in one other.

DARE TO PAIR

Just as sweet as your demeanor when you smile at that newbie mom who is clearly judging you with an implied, "I'm not going to do that!" **Bless Your Heart** wine is a light and crisp Georgia Muscadine, by 12 Spies Vineyards, exploding with fruit flavors that will remind you to live and *let live.* Relax on your porch swing with your new-mom pal and sip on this sweet dessert wine with a light finish and hinting of crisp green apple. After a glass or two, you'll both be a little more understanding of one another.

Maybe I *Don't* Know Everything

A couple of days ago as I drove the kids to school, Kate said from the back seat, "The moon is the sun."

I responded to her in the manner I often do when my mind is on other things, with a dismissive, "Mmm hmm, yes."

Then I thought back to an article my husband, Mike, had

read. It said that when parents make a point to intellectually challenge their children outside of school and take advantage of educational opportunities wherever they exist, those children become more successful than children with parents, well, like me. (The author didn't mention me by name, of course, but I'm pretty sure it was implied.)

So, with the article in mind, I decided that Kate deserved a better response than the one I had given her.

"Actually, Kate," I said. "The moon is a moon and the sun is a star."

"What, Mama? What is a moon?"

Dang. I don't really know what a moon is.

"The moon is a moon, kind of like a satellite, but the sun is a big, hot star."

"The sun is a star?"

Oh, Lord, here it comes. She's going to ask me what the difference is between a star and a satellite. How the hell am I going to explain that to a four-year-old when I don't really know the answer? I still can't get it through my head that Pluto is no longer a planet!

"Well, yes, honey, it's our brightest star," I began, now second-guessing if the sun actually was a star and musing about whether maybe the North Star was brighter?

"It's kind of a nebulous body that gives us our light and our heat." Oh, great, like she's going to know what *nebulous* means. Do *I* know what nebulous means?

I started to kind of panic. Every time I tried to explain it in a new way, I used words or metaphors that I worried would elicit more questions from her. While I wanted to feed her thirst for knowledge, I also wanted out of the current conversation because I knew I had no hope of explaining the intricacies of the universe to her. I should've stopped, but I blundered on.

"You see, God created the earth and there was this big

bang . . ." Okay, now I'm teaching creation and evolution in one breath—and neither one very well.

"There are nine planets," (there are nine, right?) "in our solar system." What the hell does a four-year-old know about the damn solar system? Wait, there's eight now. They fired Pluto.

"We live on the planet earth and we have a moon that we call—the moon." I am an idiot.

"The planets all revolve around the sun and it keeps us warm." What if she asks me what the moon does? I don't know what the moon does.

"We've sent people up all the way to the moon before. There's an American flag (and a Tri-Delta pin so the story goes) up there." Why is my mouth still moving? At this point, I could feel perspiration on my forehead. It was becoming clear that I was too dumb to have had children. At least I *knew* I was too dumb. Most dumb people don't know they're dumb. So, I guess I had one up on *them*. I began thinking about how much worse this was going to get when the girls began bringing their homework home and asking me for help. They'd end up in remedial classes if I was the one to offer assistance. Mike was going to have to be their tutor.

I pictured the four of us sitting around the table in a few years. Mike would be explaining math or geography or something. Kate and Meg would have their books open and be listening intently. And then—pan right—there's me, furiously taking notes so as not to miss a word he was saying.

"Does any of that make sense, sweetie?" I asked a bit nervously.

Silence.

"Kate?""

I looked in the rear-view mirror and there sat Kate, earphones on, staring at the TV screen, watching *Mickey Mouse Clubhouse*.

DARE TO PAIR

As a mom, you are learning and growing all the time. You know a lot more than you give yourself credit for. For instance, you know the moon brightens up the night sky. Take a moment to admire its beauty while you take in the subtle smoke and dry wood flavors of this medium-bodied red with hints of strawberry and cherry fruit, **Alta Luna Pinot Noir**.

I Can't Accept Help

When I offer to help out a friend, I *mean* it. I was sincere when I offered to pick up Sally Jo for a playdate so you'd have some extra time to pack up your house for your big move across town. I wasn't joking when I told you I'd bring Finn to Open Gym so he could run out all of that three-year-old energy while you had some quiet time with your two-month-old. And I was dead serious when you looked like you were having a nervous breakdown, and I suggested Lucy come spend the whole day at our place so you could catch a movie and get some official me time. I am happy to help! Because I know what it's like to *need* and want help.

So then why can't *I* ever accept help?

This past week my husband and I were both sick. There were no parents around to take the kids in while we slept our colds away, no sisters or brothers to whisk them away for an hour or two. But, friends, we do have, some are the very friends I've lent a hand to in the past. Yet, for some reason though, I couldn't take them up on their offer to help.

One sweet friend asked how she could help me, "I know how hard it is when you both don't feel well. Let me know if I can do anything at all, like pick up something at the store for you."

The cold came on the heels of a weekend away in New York City so there was nothing in the house in terms of decent food. When she suggested that idea, I couldn't help but think: *Yes, please! We need all of the ingredients for chicken-noodle soup, peanut butter, bread, milk, and waffles, and, oh, let's not forget about our dog. He'll likely need more food any day now. Oh, thank goodness I have a friend like you!*

What I actually said to her was: "Thanks, that's so kind. I'll let you know if I do need anything, but we're cool for now."

Another friend wished us "get better soon" then suggested that she take both my boys even though her three children would all be at school. Now that's an offer from the heart, to give up your precious quiet time to watch someone else's children. I sat there, debating. Thoughts of a long nap were swirling deliriously in my head. I pictured myself texting her back: "You're amazing! What time can I expect you?" Instead, I wrote: "That's so sweet! Thanks for the offer. I think we'll be okay though."

It's maddening, isn't it? If I'm the one offering assistance, it drives me crazy when I know my friend isn't accepting it because she may feel like she's taking advantage or maybe because she wants to prove she can, in fact, *do it all.* So I was shocked at myself for passing up all those great offers for help, which I truly appreciated, and that, if I had taken up, I would have really benefited from. And *why?* Why do we as women do this to ourselves?

From that day on I decided to continue to support other moms by trying to be there in their times of need. But I also learned that it is just as important to accept help when it's offered. I know my friends and I are there for each other and that they'd feel good if they could help me. Just as important, though, is that it would also feel great to me to get some help when I really need it.

DARE TO PAIR

Often we get stuck in a habit, which we just don't know how to break. Sometimes it's good to reflect on what comes as second nature to you so that maybe you can make some changes. Do some reflection tonight as you enjoy a glass of the crisp and zesty **Second Nature Sauvignon Blanc**, from Australia's Dowie Doole winery. The nose blooms with grassy, lemony, and white-fleshed fruit flavors that imbue this very pale, almost water-white wine. After a glass or two of this mommy refreshment, relaxation and acceptance may just come automatically.

I Need to Watch What I Say Around These Kiddos

One day while cleaning the kitchen, I dropped a glass and, holding my breath, waited for it to shatter. It just bounced. I breathed a loud sigh of relief.

That is, until my four-year-old quipped, "Mommy, aren't you going to say, 'Oh, Shit?'"

DARE TO PAIR

When your quick slip of the tongue has you wanting to insert foot, remember *we've all* been there. Pour a glass of this dark and mysterious dry (but not too dry) red wine, **Big Mouth New Yorker**, from Marlborough Vineyards. With an abundance of ripe gooseberries and black currants, it promises bold flavors to your taste buds.

I Should Have Trusted My Gut

I was bawling my eyes out, even shaking a little—okay, a lot—I was furious! My son was only about a month old and, at close to midnight, had woken up crying. My husband firmly felt that we needed to let him "cry it out." We'd been reading that phrase in many of our parenting books lately, but I thought it was too soon. He's just too young. But I was a new mom having a hard time deciding between going with my instincts and taking what might be good advice.

Plus, with advice coming from everyone for everything, including my husband, I felt as if I was losing my mind. So in that moment, I thought maybe my husband could be right. Still I had my doubts. So far Luke wasn't the best eater. Even though he had just had a full breast-feeding session, who was to say how much he really ate? He may have fallen asleep half way through, and I might not have been paying attention. Truthfully, I was snuggling with him, but also watching *American Idol*. I wasn't noticing his every swallow. Maybe he's going through a growth spurt so he needs more?

I couldn't take it! I'd probably let that poor little boy cry for thirty minutes before I broke down and ran in to get him as I cried, feeling horrible that I could let him suffer like that. I immediately offered him milk. He ate furiously! Is he starving? He is, isn't he? I'm the worst mom ever!

That's a night that even my husband realized we made the wrong call. Now we know it was just too early, way too early, to let him cry it out. Since then I've learned to trust my motherly instincts rather than books and advice.

DARE TO PAIR

Motherly instinct or women's intuition? Either way, those days when you know you need to trust in *you* and you get it right, reach for a bottle of Bergevin Lane Vineyards' **Intuition Reserve Red Wine**. It will awaken *all* your senses with powerful aromas of cassis, dark fruits, blueberries, and lavender.

There's a Dangerous Array of Toys Cluttering My Floors

I used to walk around the house naked. Back when my husband and I were newlyweds with no kids or drop-in company, I loved the freedom and sexiness of strutting around in the nude doing basic tasks—starting the coffee in the morning, tossing in some laundry after a post-workout shower, or just because it was in-between the work and lounge clothes in the evening.

Ten years later, I don't leave my bedroom with any part of me naked, right down to my feet. Shoes are a key part of my home wear these days and I have one pair that is actually called my "house" shoes. It is not that I'm ashamed of my toes or have a foot thing—I've just grown tired of stepping on things barefoot.

Three kids, five and under, plus two shedding dogs create a lot of dirt, clutter, crumbs, and hair! Our hardwood floors keep the downstairs of our home cool and attractive, but they've become disgusting to walk on anymore! I could sweep twice a day and still get crud on my feet (believe me, I've tried. I own a top-rated vacuum.) .

Worse, our carpeted stairs tend to take the brunt of the gunk. At least our home builders were wise when they picked the carpet color. Although the quality of the carpet is poor, the off-white color with little specks of other darker shades hides a lot of dirt (and yellow lab hair). And, I have learned to ignore that accumulates at the back of each step whenever I go up.

Upstairs is a different story altogether. While my bedroom, which also doubles as my office, is off-limits for toys, the kids have so many that their rooms are overflowing and they litter the rest of our second story. (Now, I'm just as guilty as any other red-blooded American for overbuying, but I'd estimate ninety percent of the toys my kids own were either gifts or hand-me-downs.) Even after having "cleaned up," there is always a bit of crayon, a solo LEGO, or small vehicle lying in wait for me to step on.

But still worse are the wet messes. My daughter enjoys using bathroom sink water to fill her play-kitchen tea cups. I try not to squelch the kid's imaginative play, but the moment I step on soggy carpet I can feel my blood pressure rise. Fortunately, potty training is over in my house, but an elderly lab means stepping in the occasional leakage or dog vomit. My dear dog saves this for the carpeted upstairs, usually a high traffic area, because it is devoid of toys and other clutter.

DARE TO PAIR

Rather than complain about the toys and clutter—find a solution! Tuck your feet into a cute pair of house shoes and fill your glass with this smooth and golden, medium-bodied wine, **Barefoot Chardonnay**. Bursting with honeyed peach and Fuji apple flavors, this wine will have your forgetting all about your barefoot days.

And although this all stresses me out, drives me to drink, makes my blood boil, and all of that, I know this too shall *pass*. Someday I'll have an immaculately clean home again because no one will be living there and I'll have all day to tidy up. I might even miss that occasional LEGO or french fry.

For now I'll wear my house shoes, try not to trip over the action figures, and let my kids be kids. And anyway, the hardwood floor is pretty chilly on bare feet first thing in the morning.

Your Child Is Bound to Embarrass You at the Pediatrician's Office

It was our routine four-year-old checkup at the pediatrician's office. The kind, young doctor seemed to take extra care as she patiently listened to my son's heartbeat, checked his ears, his tonsils, and asked me questions about his sleeping and eating habits.

I'm always proud to describe our health friendly dishes as well as with our limited TV hours. While I definitely don't qualify to be dubbed "supermom" by the local mommies group, I care about my children's health habits.

Next, the doctor palpated my son's belly button and then she pulled down his pants to examine his thighs and legs, only after explaining to him that nobody but a doctor in the company of his parents and his parents could touch his private parts. My son looked at her in interest, then at me.

"My pee-pee won't go down," he told her, matter-of-factly. She pretended to not understand him and finished up her exam.

"My penis won't go down," he said louder so she could hear.

I felt my face go red immediately. When she looked at me, I shrugged. She smiled.

Turns out, there's a lot you can't plan for when it comes to our kids' doctor's appointments. There will be one time, at least one time, when they *are* going to embarrass you. And it's likely to be one you'll not forget.

DARE TO PAIR

There's no one who can embarrass us quite like our sweet little angels can. When your children bare it all for the world to see, pick up a bottle of this juicy and refreshing **Simply Naked Moscato**, a sweetly balanced, unoaked wine with floral notes and flavors of orange marmalade, peach and honey. We guarantee you this: we've *all* been there.

Chicks Really Do Dig Scars!

Early in his life, our son Carter had to have major surgery that left a major scar across his belly. Whenever the scar came up because he seemed to feel self-conscious about it, we would tell him "chicks dig scars." Since it's kind of an adult concept, we laughed this little piece of advice off, not thinking it would actually stick with him in any concrete way.

One day I was shopping at Golfsmith with my husband and Carter, then six-years-old. I noticed him talking with a little girl who was around seven or eight by the mini putting greens in the store. Then he walked over to me. "Mommy, I want to show her my scar."

I nodded, wondering how this demonstration would go. We couldn't go back on what we'd always told him now! What was about to happen could be part of his healing process—learning to be proud of everything he'd made it through and open to talking about it. What's more learning to accept his body and what came with the surgery. I felt proud of my son.

I watched as he lifted up his shirt to show her.

"Cool!" She exclaimed. "How'd you get that?"

My son's little face lit up as he explained about the surgery. I let them play and talk for about the next thirty minutes, observing how he totally ate up talking to her—an older girl to boot. She was totally *into* it!

While we'd originally used what we'd told him about his scars as a way to soothe his fears, my husband and I marveled at its truth.

DARE TO PAIR

As moms, we often forget how closely our children do listen to us. Most times, this is good and sometimes, not so good. Forgive the mistakes knowing next time you'll try to remember your little ones are around with the pale **(oops) Sauvignon Blanc**, from Chilean winery Viña Underraga. With green undertones and intense, fruit aromas that unveil a crisp taste of delicate citrus, you'll do better next time.

Sometimes You Just Have to Work with What You've Got

Admit it! You know you've done some crazy things to get your little ones to sleep, make them laugh, or simply to entertain them while you're waiting to pay the bill after a surprisingly well-behaved dinner at Outback Steakhouse. So some of the things I and other moms resort to in order to soothe our children just doesn't surprise me.

I've never been one to remember lyrics to songs; even the simplest nursery rhyme wouldn't come to mind when my first was born. I had "Twinkle, Twinkle Little Star" and "You Are My Sunshine" down, but there was no doubt I needed more in my repertoire.

While rocking my four-week-old to sleep one day, one of my college sorority songs belted surprisingly out of my mouth. Excited that I could remember at least one song, I sang it over and over. By the time my son finally shut his eyes, I'd transformed the song by replacing a few of the words so it pertained more to me and my baby. For more than a year, it has been part of our nightly playlist of mommy songs.

Did I mention that a voice coach at my college had point-blank told me that I should lip-synch the songs because my voice wasn't working for her? I admit, I already knew the truth, but it stung anyway! Regardless, my son acts like he enjoys my voice and, once he started talking, he would actually beg for, "One more song, Mommy!" Take *that*, voice coach!

One day while we were watching *Go, Diego, Go!* the main character announced he was on a hunt for an anaconda. I was catapulted right back to the '90s, particularly to Sir-Mix-A-Lot's anthem "Baby Got Back," which has a line about an anaconda, so I started to joyfully sing it. Although my son looked at me like I was nuts, I enjoyed every minute of it. And as kids do, he continually asks me to repeat that "Diego song" whenever the snake is mentioned on the show. So now he's rapping along with me.

That song isn't exactly a children's tune, but I was relieved to hear that a friend had the same dilemma when her daughter was a baby. She was always struggling to remember lyrics to lullabies. Then one night, after more than an hour of trying to get her little girl to sleep, she crooned to her a lullaby version of Justin Timberlake's "Sexy Back." The melody sent her daughter off to dreamland.

Whether it's a monologue from *Bridesmaids* or the theme

song to *America's Next Top Model* ("Wanna be on Top?"), use what you've got to soothe your children. You may discover it works.

DARE TO PAIR

We may not have voices that would dazzle the *American Idol* judges, but at least we work with what we've got. (I'd like to see those contestants try to calm a squawking child at two in the morning!) When you're all sung out, we recommend the racy and polished **14 Hands Winery's Hot to Trot**, a red blend with aromas of cherry and red currant, and supported by a frame of refined tannins that give way to subtle notes of baking spice.

We're *Only* Responsible for Teaching Lessons That Will Last a Lifetime

"Grace," our son said proudly with fingers intertwined. We probably shouldn't have, but we laughed. We had only been saying grace at our dinner table for a few weeks. Instead of doing the "Bless us, oh Lord, and these thy gifts" blessing I had been raised with, my husband and I decided to start our own tradition of grace by simply giving thanks. We didn't know how long it would take to catch on, but we were ready to give it a shot with our three-year-old and a twenty-two-month-old since they both seemed to be picking up on so much so fast lately. We were three weeks into our new routine when our preschooler volunteered to say grace.

My husband encouraged him, "Great Gavin! Go ahead, *you* say grace tonight." And he said it, so purely, so *bluntly:*

"Grace." And as I said, it was so cute we couldn't help but laugh. It was beautiful and he was proud. Then almost on cue, we all clapped.

The next night he said it again and this time we invited him to continue, "Say what you are thankful for." Sure we helped him out and gave him ideas: "You could be thankful for your family, your brother, your food, your home . . ."

He got it immediately. "I'm thankful for my Mommy. My Daddy. My bruddah," he announced as he looked at each one of us around the table. Then he glanced down and said, "I'm thankful for my doggie . . ." He paused in a slump, having run out of living and breathing blessings. Then, with a charge of excitement he concluded, ". . . and I'm thankful for my ambulance"—his new *favorite* toy. He smiled.

Impressed, my husband and I looked at one another and then back at him and said, "Amen!" He repeated it back to us while his little brother said his best two-year-old amen. Then we clapped and told Gavin what a great job he had done and gave his little bro some props, too, for his participation.

A week later, at Christmas Eve dinner with Grandma and Grandpa, he again suggested: "Grace." Now he was doing it just to get attention and a hearty laugh from his dad, which was delivered on cue. But he did again follow it up with being thankful for each of us at the table, even Grandpa *twice.* Then, out of the blue, he said he's thankful for his Aunt Lisa who actually couldn't join us that year. (In all fairness, he may not exactly remember her, but he hears her name often and had, undoubtedly, heard it earlier in the day.)

Then, the grand finale, "And I am thankful for my penis." Well, *who* could argue with that!

* * *

Though sometimes it may not feel that way, I know my efforts as a mom will have a great impact on my children's lives. I *know* this, but the results still astonish me at times. Ultimately, whether or not saying grace becomes something that they do in their lives, they *will* be learning to be aware of what they are grateful for. As my husband and I try to lead by example and show our children how many things there are to be grateful for—be it family, food on the table, toys, or even an event, or a feeling—it is our hope that they will start to have an appreciation of what enriches their lives rather than to just take things for granted.

The brilliant part of all of this isn't that a three-year-old is hamming it up in front of family, or that it's cute that he's thankful for his penis, a toy or a missed aunt; but rather it's seeing that he got what we were trying to teach him. Sometimes it is the simple lessons that can last a lifetime. But they have to start somewhere and be nurtured—ultimately, it's up to *us* to deliver grace. As we watch our kids take it in, we have one more thing to be grateful for. *Amen!*

DARE TO PAIR

Tonight, as you unwind from the day and reminisce about all the ways your children are growing and learning, enjoy a glass of **Grace Family Vineyards Cabernet Sauvignon**. We suspect that after experiencing this creamy Cab with its intense black currant and dry black cherry with plum, your taste buds will be giving thanks.

Today, I Chose Not to Rush My Kids

Tears flowed from my eyes as I read these lines:

"Let me tell you what had become of me.
My distractions:
Excessive phone use, commitment overload, multiple
page to-do lists, and the pursuit of perfection consumed
me. And yelling at the people I loved was a direct result
of the loss of control I was feeling in my life."

So wrote author Rachel Macy Stafford in her blog post titled, "The Important Thing about Yelling" (handsfreemama .com). The words made me cry because of how much I identified with her. It seems there are not enough hours in the day—even when I wake up at 5:30 am and don't fall asleep until 11:00 pm. There just never seems to be enough time.

Work. Cleaning. Meals. Meal *planning*. Grocery shopping. Errands. Playdates. Oh, and maybe a decent conversation or two with my husband. Friends. *What friends?*

Also hanging over my head are all the other things I'd like to take care of such as organizing two years' worth of photos and making that video montage I've been talking about for so long. I need to register my son for pre-k and make a dentist appointment for myself. And the school photos, framed in the hall, are still from last year while the new school photos, taken three months ago already, are still sitting on my desk waiting to be framed. Meanwhile, I dream about the next book I want to write, the next *three*, actually.

In between all of this, I squeeze in quality time with my sons, wanting to embrace every second of their smiles and joy, the feeling of their hugs, the sound of their little voices. And what's *always* on my mind is how to make their lives better and what more can I do for them. I need more *time*.

Sometimes I want to scream for more time or break down

and cry. And I know it's because, so often, I feel like everything is out of control. Out of *my* control. And this is when I lose my patience. For example, when we are running late and I turn around to see that my three-year-old has decided to strip nude. Or, when the house is finally clean and my four-year-old has thrown every single toy out of his toy box in search of his police costume that must be worn *right now*. And, when I'm always saying, "Just give me a second" and the second turns into an hour.

That author bestowed a message of hope upon me at an incredible time. It was a wake-up call, if you will. Her parting words fill me with power to drop what doesn't matter and focus on what really does:

> *"The important thing is . . . life is too short to get upset over spilled cereal and misplaced shoes.*
> *The important thing is . . . no matter what happened yesterday, today is a new day.*
> *Today we can choose a peaceful response.*
> *And in doing so, we can teach our children that peace builds bridges—bridges that can carry us over in times of trouble."*
> *Inspired, I know that today is a new day for us all. And I will make a conscious effort to find simplicity by enjoying the small and important and letting go of distraction—today, I choose to build bridges.*

DARE TO PAIR

When you let go of the irrelevant distractions, suddenly and conspicuously you will find peace. **Harmony Cellars Chardonnay** will bring you fully into the present as it awakens your senses with prominent aromas of citrus, apple, and butterscotch. Sweet, buttery and creamy—relaxation will be your only distraction.

CHAPTER 9

Savoring and Grateful

Often, it's the simple, small things in our lives that make us the most grateful. They can take the form of the contentment that comes when the kids are finally peacefully napping or when the family is laughing hysterically together, or just simply when you realize those little beings have deeply embedded themselves in your heart.

Just as wine should be sipped not gulped, savor those precious, yet fleeting moments. With the pour also comes a moment to pause, to reflect, and to be grateful for all that you do have.

The Years Go By So Fast

We moved into a new house when Nathan was about two-and-a-half. His room had a window, which he loved to look out of, yet wasn't tall enough to reach. I remember him constantly asking me to pick him up so he could see outside, and it never crossed my mind that he'd ever be big enough to see out of that window by himself.

Sometime after Nathan turned five, I was walking by his

room and there he stood looking out that window. I immediately started bawling, wondering: where did the time go? It seemed like just yesterday that I was hoisting him up, thinking I'd be doing it for eternity.

As I lay in bed drifting off that night, I found myself abruptly shaken by math. Yes, math. In 9 years, my husband will be 50, I calculated. That didn't seem far off at all, considering how quickly the years go by these days. Then I did some more math: nine plus five is 14. My son will be 14 in nine years. Fourteen! That's just nine more Christmases and birthdays, which didn't seem like nearly enough! This is when pure and utter panic set in.

Earlier that day, we'd had a family medical emergency, which made the whole day a whirlwind tizzy of emotion and phone calls. It seemed every request such as "please come draw with me" or "will you play with me, mama?" was met with: "In just a sec, honey, I have to make a call" or "I can't sweetie, I have to figure this out."

Now a kind of dread was washing over me, suffocating me. There will be a time when I'm not being begged to read to them or tuck them in at night. The time may come when they no longer want to "help" me prepare dinner. There will be a time when I'm not pouring their milk or buttoning their pants or brushing their hair anymore. One day, when I go to give them a kiss I won't have to bend over or they might even dodge it.

These years that my sons truly are little boys have been going by so fast and will continue to do so. They probably won't even last until they are 14. Even sooner than that, my sons may decide that their friends are more worthy of their attention than I am. I will suddenly have all the free time I could dream of and long for their pestering me for attention, asking questions, and needing me to cuddle.

Stricken, I realized how the past five years have gone by in a blur; and the quote: "The days are long, the years are short," burned in my mind. After I was finally able to catch my breath and I came to terms with the bittersweet process of letting go, which is the most inevitable part of parenthood, I was so thankful. I was thankful to have had such a powerful insight to remind me how precious each moment of each day is. No matter the messes, the endless questions, the early wake-up times—even the sass—I am so blessed to have had this realization before it's too late.

This is a reminder to slow down. Slow it down and enjoy each magical moment that comes with each crazy stage of childhood. Look over at your child right this very moment. Whatever he or she is doing, that's what's most important. Take a break, and join in his or her world. And while you're playing or drawing or creating with her, look deeply into her eyes and, not with your iPhone's camera, capture them in your mind forever, just the way they are. When you kiss him goodnight, and brush your fingers through his hair, breathe in the child he is today. Savor every moment.

DARE TO PAIR

In the crush of motherhood's responsibilities, we have all thought that we'd always be kissing our babies good night. When you're hit with the bittersweet realization that your kids are growing up and will leave you one day, try the refreshing rosé-like **Butterfly Kiss Pinot Grigio**, by The Wine Bar. It will not only smooth away the sadness, it will also have you celebrating all the butterfly kisses of your children's childhood.

My Kids Napped Today—Victory!

It's 12:31 p.m. in the afternoon on a hot Saturday at the beginning of summer. For the first time since 6:00 a.m., the house is quiet. Not *really* quiet because the dishwasher and dryer are running simultaneously and I did turn on the Singers & Swing music channel. But there's a respite from the hustle and bustle of "Mommy" this and "Mommy" that. There's a quiet that stems from my two boys *not* fighting and bickering with one another and from my youngest toddler *not* trying to climb up on the dining room table and then hollering out "Mama! Mama!" with his arms outstretched for me to catch him mid-air, just so he can do it over and over again.

It's a blissful quiet. There's a peace in knowing that they are contentedly asleep, snuggled in their beds, and that it's the calm before the storm of our afternoon, which will be busy with friends and fun in the pool, and our evening, which will be bustling as we attempt to successfully knock out our bedtime routine with two exhausted boys. But for now, it's quiet.

DARE TO PAIR

Ahhh, when the little ones go down so easily for their naps, instinctively you want to reach for your bottle of **Happy Camper Merlot**. Then you remember it's early afternoon and there's still a long list of chores to complete. So until tonight, your taste buds will have to wait for the smooth taste of Blackberry, plum, and spice.

I'm torn between napping myself and getting some work done. Of course, even more housework comes to mind—but no, not today. It's Saturday, and the thought of doing another round of bathroom cleanings just to see them blanketed in towels, floaties, SpongeBob undies and miscellaneous shorts and shirts—no, thank you.

I'm not going to use this amazing hour or two for that (dear God, *please* let it be two hours). I'm going to enjoy it. I think I'll pour a glass of iced tea, relax on the sofa with a book and listen to a little Sinatra. After a crazy and frustrating morning, these blissful moments of mommyhood are to be savored.

As My Children's Interests Flourish, I Grow Too

Until I had children I was confident in my drawing skills, at least for the purposes of drawing something basic like a flower or houses with grey smoke curling from the chimney or a cowboy hat (this last developed about the time I decided to go to college just outside of Music City USA). But those three things are pretty much all I could draw. Even my stick figures end up coming out looking strange.

In the last year, however, my skills have been challenged. My four-year-old demanded that I draw him a police car with a bad guy in the back. You can do this, I coached myself. So first I drew two tires. Then before I could draw the body of the car, "No, mom, that's not how you do it!" he said, looking at me like I *knew* I was doing it all wrong.

"Well, how do you want me to do it?" I inquired.

"You know, the way it's *supposed* to go." He explained.

After a few failed attempts, I had finally had myself a pretty good-looking cop car with the freakiest female police officer driving it. My human-figure attempts aren't good at all. This goes back to a time in seventh-grade art class when we were asked to draw a picture of our partners. My partner *was* an artist. And she did an exceptional job of creating a remarkable likeness of me on paper. I, on the other hand, made her look like something between a frog and a pie. I think it was at that very moment that I just accepted it: *I am not an artist; I cannot draw.* Whenever he asks me to draw something, I may start it, but pretty soon he takes over.

While his new passion is being pursued, we encourage his imagination to flourish. Although we give in to his repeated requests to draw police car after police car, we also suggest to him, "What else can we think of that would be cool to draw today?" And Luke also gets to spend some time drawing with both me and with his dad. He's learning technique and form from his father, but we both bring a little imagination to the table too. I'll take a recent experience and use everything in me to bring it to life on paper.

Recently, I insisted we color an "under-the-sea" picture. So I started with a few colorful fish and he added one. I asked him what else should be in the picture. He wanted to see a jelly-fish, stingray, and shark. I worked those in. Then I drew a tiny fish that was about to be eaten by the shark and said, "Poor little fish." Luke didn't like hearing this.

"We need to save him! Draw a scuba diver saving him." He implored.

I did, plus a boat with an anchor. Though I must tell you I'm afraid that the shark will get it, too. What was really happening was that we created a story while he and I practiced drawing. The result was a beautiful masterpiece of us working together, creating.

I used to become frustrated trying to figure out how to draw the things my boys were asking to see. Now, though, I look forward to developing my abilities while having a rich sharing experience with my children and an up-close view into their interests. It's an exciting journey observing the evolution of a human being—and the artist in Mommy just *may* be progressing as well.

> ## DARE TO PAIR
>
> When your children have excited your creativity, pour a glass of **Madonna Magnum**, from Artiste Winery. Its label alone is a work of art, from a painting of the Madonna by Matti Berglund. Half Petite Sirah and half Merlot this wine boasts a wide array of dried herbs and flowers combined with black pepper, fresh earth, and licorice, followed by brambleberry jam, currents, black pepper, mildly toasted oak, and mulling spices. You'll find yourself inspired by both the wine and its label.

My Son Got to Experience Something Magical

In the same way a thrill would surge through me if Julia Roberts or Jennifer Aniston walked into a room and talked to me, I could see my little boy's eyes light up with wonder and excitement one day when there he stood: Batman, his *idol*. (Ethan won't leave the house without one of his three Batman shirts on.) But, it wasn't just any Batman; this Batman stood eye-to-eye with my three-year-old. Entranced, without even looking up at me, my son grabbed my hand and squeezed. "Mama, it's Batman! I want to play with him," he said in a hushed voice.

"Go ahead, sweetheart. I know he'd love to play with you too." I nudged my outgoing boy toward the little blondie dressed head-to-toe in a smart Batman ensemble.

My son froze. I'd never seen him like this! *Shy!* This is the same boy who walks up to complete strangers (under my supervision, of course) and asks, "How was your holiday?" after having heard my husband and I say it over and over again during the first weeks of the New Year. But here, in the front room of Charleston's Children's Museum, was a three-foot tall superhero that my son was nervous to approach. I knelt down to him and reminded him that he was a little boy just like him, who just happened to be dressed in a costume.

At that moment, mini Batman walked up to Ethan, smiled and said, "I'm Ollie, what's your name?" I nodded at his mom in gratitude, who was behind this sudden introduction.

"You can race with this one," Ollie instructed Ethan as he handed him a green golf ball. The two boys raced golf balls through the room's obstacle course. Such fun!

About twenty-minutes later, my son told me he had to go potty, so I grabbed my youngest-son Zealand's hand and followed Ethan to the restroom. When we returned—gasp!—Batman was *nowhere* to be found.

"Where's Ollie?!" Ethan asked, panic ringing in his voice.

"I'm not sure honey. Maybe he went home," I replied.

But that was not an acceptable answer to my preschooler. He was unwilling to go home until we found Ollie. We spent the next twenty minutes searching every room, but we found no sign of him. We were running late to meet friends at CiCi's Pizza, so I suggested maybe Batman had gone there—who knows, he *could* be there. This seemed to work for Ethan so we headed out the front doors of the museum. About a block up from our car, we could see Batman climbing into his mom's minivan. They drove west on King. And just like that, they disappeared into the city and we never saw Ollie again.

Ethan would talk about his mysterious friend, sometimes sadly, sometimes wonderingly, but I think what he truly remembered was that that morning had been magical for him. However he sorted the connection between Batman and Ollie in his mind, for him Ollie was a blessing because when he saw Ollie he recognized a soulmate. I felt so gifted that day to experience my son enjoying a moment of magic in his life. Even if only for that small bit of time, he found his soul's friend—something that we all wish for. Though these encounters may be few and far between, I wish him many, many more.

DARE TO PAIR

DARE TO PAIR: Early childhood is an *impressionable* time. So it's a tremendous blessing to watch our children experience whatever magic it is that sets their hearts racing and lets their spirits soar. With these moments, celebrate life with a glass of the sweet, white **Dreamer Sauvignon Blanc**, which boasts of grapes, pleasing nuances of honey, and tropical fruit that lead to a smooth finish.

I Love Discovering Who My Children Are

It's crazy how different two children's personalities can be, even when they share the same parents. I remember my Mom would always talk about how my sister, brother, and I had totally distinct characteristics. I wouldn't come to realize what she meant until I had my own children.

My husband and I have watched our daughter and our son flourish over the years, as they become who they will each be as people. We had our daughter first, and that little girl never wanted for anything: clothes, toys, shows, hair bows, Disney movies, she had it all. Because we had pampered her, we prepared ourselves for a bit of jealousy when she was three and her brother came along. Yet, we were surprised at how loving and unselfish she was toward him.

My son is evolving into quite the hilarious little man, with a sense of humor so big none of us can stop laughing. He's strong willed, bullheaded, and tough. I know we'll never have to worry about him; he's a leader, not a follower. The only issue is dealing with having to fight him tooth and nail on every single little thing he doesn't want to do. It can be exhausting.

Probably the only way my children are alike is that my daughter is also a strong-willed little girl. She knows what she wants and goes for it. She can negotiate any unknowing adult into three cookies when they've clearly only approved one. She, too, is a leader, able to convince most of her friends to play the same dress-up game for the hundredth time—where she is the queen and her friends are the peasants.

It's also interesting to watch when she shows interest in boys and how unglued she becomes every time one comes around. It's as if the leader in her disappears, replaced by a googly-eyed follower. Everything boys say is hilarious, and every game they want to play is suddenly her favorite.

My daughter seems to need more attention than our son does. Sometimes it feels as though all I do is try to build her up and make her feel loved and nurtured, while my son smiles and goes about his own business. He doesn't need anyone to make him feel good about himself. Additionally, while my daughter is constantly asking for someone to come over to play with her, he's great at entertaining himself with his toys.

When my son is unhappy about something, he'll pout for a minute then go about his way. For example, even though he can be incredibly stubborn, like sitting at the dinner table until bedtime instead of eating his broccoli, once the fight is over, he doesn't let it affect the way he feels about himself or life.

Meanwhile, our daughter can have a more negative or dramatic approach to life at times. When one bad thing happens, she goes to extremes, deciding that she hates school and has no friends, even though we clearly know this isn't true. If she has a fight with her brother and we intervene, she'll say we hate her and are too hard on her.

I relish watching my children as they grow from tiny babies into miniature human beings—becoming the little people they are destined to become. One thing is certain, they are definitely very different beings. Every day, I'm intrigued to learn their likes and dislikes and the things that give them joy as well as frustrate them. I know I have no control over any of it. While I sometimes want to intercede and help them by sharing my experience and giving advice, I know I shouldn't. They need to evolve on their own and gain their own experience. I'm learning that each day with them is a gift and that we're raising them to be fine human beings, idiosyncrasies and all.

DARE TO PAIR

Our children are going to be who they are destined to become. Their characteristics can be as varied as words with the entire alphabet—Amazing, Brilliant, on to Zany. Accept and toast how unique your children are with this juicy and well-rounded **A to Z Chardonnay**. Its bright and fruity aromas such as kiwi, tangerine, and pear will help you savor and be grateful for your children just the way they are.

Summer Vacation at the Beach Sure Has Changed

This year, for our annual vacation with my husband's family, we went to St. George Island, Florida. I absolutely love it! It isn't crowded. It's quaint. There's great seafood, of course; what beach doesn't have great seafood? I'm never more relaxed than when I am at the beach. I could sit on the sand under an umbrella with the waves crashing and the breeze blowing every day for the rest of my life and not feel as though

I'm missing anything. It's just calming and serene, quite the break from reality.

It's funny how a trip to the beach evolves during the course of your life. When you are a kid, it's all about impatiently waiting for your parents to drink their coffee or do whatever it is they do before they take you out to play in the surf. It took *forever!* Once you find your spot on the beach, you spend the day riding and jumping in the waves and making sandcastles, which never look like the ones built by the show-offs down the beach who somehow manage to sculpt a palace.) Or you methodically unfurl your kite and launch it proudly into the air only to realize that kite flying isn't all that exciting.

As a teen, you're there for one reason and one reason *only:* to get a tan. You are out on the sand before anyone else in the morning and stay there long after everyone else has grown tired of the sand sticking to their skin. Every day, you check your tan lines to see if they are more drastic than they were the day before.

When you are an adult and before you have had your children, you finally notice how beautiful the water and surrounding scenery of the beach really are. It becomes a place of respite for you instead of play. Now the focus of a beach vacation is more on what you will be eating and drinking there, which is sure to include plenty of margaritas. Your biggest job is to make sure you're not out of Bloody Mary mix for your "it's five o' clock somewhere" happy hour.

When you're on an adults-only vacation by the sea and you notice other people with babies, you marvel at how difficult it must be to tend to a baby at all times while on vacation. It's *quite* the birth control, actually.

Then comes the day when you have your own family. Suddenly, the trip is mainly about how it's not really *your* trip anymore. You can't stay on at the beach until the sun begins to go down, relaxing with an adult beverage. Adult beverage? Ha! How about sippy cups and sunscreen? You've got naps to monitor and bottles to prepare. What's a book?

Yes, vacations sure aren't what they used to be. Yet no matter how truly relaxing the trips once were or how enjoyable the Margaritas consumed in peace and quiet with a *People* magazine were—it's so very special to spend summer vacations with my family at the beach. Seeing my children's joy as they learn to love the ocean as much as I do, I realize that, when the kids have grown and left, I'll still hear my children's laughter in the echo of the crashing waves.

DARE TO PAIR

Sure, vacations are fun for us mommies in a different way *these days*. When you're longing for those summer vacations that were a bit more carefree and wild, reminisce with a glass of Fiesta Winery's **Skinny Dippin Sweet White Wine**. The distinct apple flavor of this light, mildly sweet white is sure to whisk you back to another time, *if only temporarily*.

They Call It Like It Is

Our family was having dinner one night and my four-year-old son, Dominick, was burping loudly. My husband Doug asked him sternly, "Dominick, what do you say?"

Dominick responded, "Excuse me!"

I rolled my eyes. "It's like having a dinosaur at the table!"

Doug said, "Yeah, a Burpasaurus!"

We laughed; then Dominick leaned over to me and whispered, "Mommy, you should call Daddy a Fartasaurus"

DARE TO PAIR

A deep, ruby red with rich, concentrated dark-cherry, plum, and floral-spice aromas, New Zealand's **Hāhā Pinot Noir** is the perfect wrap to a day of laughter. Actually, *hāhā* means savory and luscious in Maori. The black fruit flavors and silky smooth texture all lead to a very satisfying, dry finish.

Nighttime

At long last it is night, the entire house quiet except for the white noise of his small fan, my son's precious lips are allowing sweet small breaths to exit his dreaming body. His blue satin blanket is laced between his fingers and propped across the side of his face. Growing faster than ever, his long legs are stretched almost the length of his mattress. The strands of his exquisite blonde hair (rare in our family) frame his 18-month-old face.

The three meltdowns and the spilled juice on our freshly steamed carpet earlier in the day are almost a distant memory. His endless "no's" to all my requests seem less frustrating now as I look down on my sleeping son.

Who is this little person? Who is this being that my husband and I lovingly created? In the madness of the daytime, I never have time to visit these questions, to really take in the full magnitude of what it is to be a parent: every lesson taught, every kiss sealed onto their foreheads, every "I love you" realized.

You are shaping who they are with every second of the day. And isn't it amazing how the love can rise above all the chaos and stress of each day making it all so very right?

When looking at my son, I see his body curled comfortably in his bed, after he's expended all of his high-voltage energy, and now I see the depth and the magic of his being.

The image of her child in slumber calls forth the mystical delight in being a mom like no other.

DARE TO PAIR

After you kiss your angel good night, end the day on just the right note. Indulge in the sweet, fruit-forward flavors of **Angel Vine Zinfandel Columbia Valley**–blackberry, red and black raspberry and spice. With a nose of dried tea, chocolate, and dark berries, it, together with your darlings' slumbering forms, will remind you that sometimes simply being a mom is *heavenly*.

CHAPTER 10

Celebrating

*W*hile wine offers different things to different women, what is true is that we often take a sip from the glass to celebrate the larger milestones of life. You remember the first time you and your friends splurged and ordered "by the bottle" at your favorite restaurant, the Spanish red you drank on the night you got engaged, and the first sip you took after you finally finished nursing your first-born child. For moms, there are so many watersheds to celebrate. Sometimes we celebrate to acknowledge the good in our lives. Other times a celebration is in order when we've moved through a challenge and can breathe in a sigh of relief that it has been overcome.

This chapter's stories are about the simple, yet huge, things in our lives that make us realize how very lucky we are and that a party is *definitely* in order.

We Tried Almost Everything to Conceive

There are 16 pregnancy tests under my bathroom sink.

Waiting. Teasing. Taunting. Begging me to take one.

Next to them are the perfectly packaged ovulation kits starring a toothless, cherubic baby on the side smiling, calling out to me: "I could be yours! I love you!" But, as each month goes by, I can read my body and can tell that my period is imminent. I sigh with hope that one day I will need them all. And I *will* take all of them to make sure the first one isn't a false-positive—which is a cruel joke. When the time comes, I want to know that I am pregnant *for sure.* But until that day, I continue to toss each bonus pregnancy test that comes with all of my ovulation kits into my collection.

Having a family was always my dream. I knew I had to be good at it—it's in my *genes.* I come from a family of six and a long line of fertile women. When my gynecologist told me that it wasn't physically possible for me to get pregnant unless I had surgery, I was crushed. The surgery would cost $45,000, yet insurance wasn't going to cover it. At that point, the devastating thought occurred to me that having biological children might not be in the cards for me.

Pretty much immediately, the number of pregnant women and parents I saw bloomed. They were *everywhere*, at the park, at the mall, walking down the street. I found myself studying them. Analyzing them. *Judging* them. I would think that, if we had kids, ours would be better behaved or we could provide for them better financially or our kids would be way smarter. I'd never thought of myself as a jealous person, but I found these feelings creeping into my soul, lurking—and I hated it.

A few months later, after my husband and I had changed health insurance, we learned that it covered the surgery I needed to correct infertility! We were so excited. I had a blockage in my left fallopian tube, which had to be removed because the eggs could not come down to the uterus for fertilization. My reproductive endocrinologist felt confident that this removal would fix my infertility. I immediately set up the surgery date.

After surgery, we thought that getting pregnant would be easy since everything was technically fixed. I felt like I was on cloud nine! All our dreams of kids and a family would come true! We started using ovulation kits to help us with conception, but they posed a bigger challenge than we thought. Then after months of frustration, impatience and tears, we started on Clomid, a drug that induces ovulation.

Clomid made me feel crazy. It felt like my hormones were on overdrive. I felt emotional. I felt bloated. I felt like my body was about to experience the biggest, most massive, explosive period of my life. But no, it was just the Clomid. I felt in my soul that this was the answer and dealt with the side effects with a forced smile. We knew that there was a chance for a multiple-birth pregnancy with that drug, but we were willing to take the chance. We were ready.

After six months, a handful of money, numerous ovulation kits, two rounds of artificial insemination and these little white pills, I was done. I wasn't medically allowed to take any more Clomid and we were still not pregnant.

By this time, we were talking about how long we would continue with medical intervention. We talked about adoption. We talked about our relationship, love, commitment, and our dreams. Even though it was stressful, we were a team. These talks only made me love my husband more, love *us* more. We talked about what we should do next: nothing, hormone injections, or in vitro fertilization.

The first night I had to inject the hormones into my stomach, I couldn't do it. My husband carefully cleaned my stomach with an alcohol pad, I looked away, and it was done. It didn't physically hurt— what hurt was the idea that this was our reality. It wasn't what I'd *planned*. This was not what I had in mind. I saw myself pregnant and glowing—on my own schedule.

After a few months of hormone injections, numerous ultra-sounds, spontaneous trips to Denver to see the reproductive endocrinologist, and another round of artificial insemination, I was again done. We decided to stop all intervention for a while and start figuring out how to pay for in vitro fertilization. We decided we needed to get away from all of it and unwind.

It sounds so cliché, but I got pregnant naturally, while on vacation, two months later. We heard from so many people, "Relax, it will happen" and "It will happen when it's meant to happen." At the time, I wanted to scream: Shut up! You don't know what it's like to go through this! And they don't—no one does, unless they've gone through it themselves. It's hard, stressful and emotional—and, as it turns out, worth it.

When I finally mustered up the courage to take a preg-nancy test, it was *positive*. Then I took a second one just to make sure. I wasn't sure whether I should laugh and jump for joy or cry to relieve all the stress from the previous months. With great pleasure, I threw the rest of the tests that were stashed under the sink away. My husband and I had done it, together: we'd conquered the odds against us and we were so unbelievably happy.

DARE TO PAIR

We women are not only strong—we are resilient. When you have yet again overcome an obstacle that life has sent your way, take a moment to celebrate your hard-won victory. Pour a glass of this Shiraz, **Carmen Stevens' Angel's Reserve**. Its bold flavor, with plum, vanilla, spice, and hints of smoke, will remind you what you are made of.

I've Never Seen My Daughter Smile So Big

Oh, that smile! It was worth feeling like a stalker for having followed my daughter's bus to school.

I had always assumed that, when it was time for kindergarten, my kids would be driven to school. I'd just heard too many stories of bad things happening on the bus. My husband would tell me, "We rode the bus and we turned out fine," yet I couldn't help but think that the world is different now. Fights. Sexual acts. Bad drivers. All on the bus. And what about the bad guys who kidnap kids at gunpoint? Okay, okay, I know that's extreme and I can't live life in fear, but I'm supposed to protect my children—especially my baby girl Isabella.

The first week of school, as planned, I drove her. In the morning, I'd walk her to her class. In the afternoon, I sat for an hour in the feels-like-112-degree heat in a line of cars filled with moms on their phones, waiting and sweating—no AC, otherwise my car would overheat in the standstill. Then inch by inch, I'd pull forward to pick up my little one.

She was having a blast in her new role as kindergartner. She would come home beaming, sharing with us the lessons and the excitements of the day. So far, she had three boyfriends, Carson, Zachary, and Zander W.—not the other Zander in her class, she made certain to point out.

"Can I ride the bus to school, Mom?" she asked on the way home from her fourth day of school.

"Um, well, why do you want to? Isn't it fun having mommy come pick you up?" I encouraged.

"It is fun when you do, but Lillie rides the bus, and there are lots of kids in my class who do too. Zander rides the Dolphin bus."

I wanted her to have different experiences, but I didn't know what kids were like on the buses these days. Would the driver really be as protective as a teacher if some older kids were getting tough or mouthy? I set aside my nerves that afternoon and spent an hour looking at the bus route. In the mornings, after pickup, it would literally be just 10 minutes from our stop to her school. That's not so bad. What could happen in 10 minutes? And it's not as if she'd be riding with middle-school thugs. Would she?

"Bella!" I called out to her. She ran over to my desk.

"What?" (When did her response to me calling her go from "what mommy?" to a straight up, almost annoyed "what?"?)

I held her hand in mine. "Okay," I said. "Tomorrow, we will follow the bus to school so I can see the route and see who is getting on the bus. If I'm okay with it all, you can take it the next day. Cool?"

"Cool!" She jumped up with her arms waving! "I'm so excited!"

So the next day, bright and early, we followed her bus—the Octopus bus—past four stops all the way to school. Yup, just a 10-minute journey. We hopped out of the car and, in front of the school, we watched as the kids climbed out of the bus and walked the path safely into the school. Easy peasy.

She was beaming. I put my hand on her shoulder and said, "Okay, if you want to ride the bus home, I'll sign you up."

"Yes! Yes, yes, yes!!" she exclaimed, her ponytail swaying with her dancing movements.

That first morning, I kissed her good-bye and told her, "I'll be waiting for you at the bus stop. Remember—Octopus Bus!

Then that afternoon, rather than waiting in that sweltering car-rider line, my youngest daughter and I strolled in the shade five houses down to the bus stop to wait for Bella. Within minutes, her bus turned the corner. The doors opened and she came out of the bus happy as could be.

"How was it?!" I asked.

"It was great! I sat next to the birthday girl and it was so fun. The bus driver is really nice," she delighted.

Relief set in and I was so happy to see her so happy and living life, experiencing.

The next morning, I walked her to her stop. It was rather nice standing with her for a few minutes talking. It was quite the difference from rushing out the door, hopping in the car, buckling up, and racing off to school with her in the backseat behind me. It was—nice.

Her bus arrived right on time and I watched her as she climbed on and received her tag from the driver. Kindergartners must sit in the first two rows, which added to my ease. She waved and smiled as they pulled away.

Quickly, I raced to my car and stealthily followed the bus. Wanting not to be noticed, I stayed a few cars back. Ten minutes later, I got out of my car and made my way to the front doors of the school to watch as they pulled up. I saw my little girl come off the bus steps with a brave yet hesitant look.

She was all on her own. Nobody was escorting her from the bus to the school.

Halfway to the entrance of the school, she noticed me. In all of my life, I don't think I've ever seen a bigger smile. It was a smile of relief to see me there, yet she seemed to understand that I was giving her the space to do it all on her own.

"You're here." She smiled.

"I knew you could do it. I just wanted to tell you to have a good day and I love you." I was kneeling down and eye to eye with her.

"I love you, mommy," she said and then kissed my cheek.

I walked her to the entrance and kissed her good-bye. I was *so happy* I had decided to show up at school that morning.

> # DARE TO PAIR
>
> When it's time to give our babies the freedom to grow, it's also time for us to celebrate the end of an era and the beginning of a new one with **Liberty Vineyards Marquette**. Rich in color with a silky finish, this wine will offer a nose of nice spice and cherry notes and a palate that's a big hug of chocolate-covered cherries.

A Husband Who Treasures Being a Daddy

My husband Todd is an amazing father to our children. Our first baby was not the best sleeper as a newborn and I was having a hard time adjusting to being sleep-deprived. As soon as Todd got home from work each day, he would take our daughter in his arms. Sometimes, he would hold her for three hours straight while she and I both slept. He wouldn't dare move for the fear of disturbing her and thus causing me to have to wake up too. He had the magic touch with her—and still does. She is full of vibrant energy and can go from zero to sixty in about three seconds, yet he has this amazing ability to talk her "off the ledge" and into her happy zone. Their father-daughter connection is just what I'd hoped they'd share and I'm counting on their bond to get us through the teen years!

Sweet and loving, Todd is also the "fun maker" in our family. An ordinary day is transformed into a special day of fun when he gets everyone to run through the sprinklers on a hot afternoon and, afterwards, gives out Popsicles. And he is the picture of patience when our son "helps" him with projects around the house. He takes the time to explain what he's doing and finds a way for our son to play a part.

I can always count on him to spark the kids' imaginations and creative play with his awesome storytelling. When I over-hear Todd telling our four-year-old son wondrous bedtime stories, I am filled with tenderness toward him. Whether it's a story about Big Tuna's adventures or Ursula's underwater escapades, my husband can spin quite a yarn. I often imagine that he honed these skills as a mischievous little boy.

So when Todd told me—on the night of our son's second birthday—that I could "talk him into" having a third child, I knew he was telling me how much he loves being a daddy and that *he* wanted one more child. And as destiny would have it, our third child, forever known as "the baby," is the spitting image of his daddy, both in looks and personality—handsome and funny.

While other women may complain about husbands who work too much or aren't involved enough with the children, I find myself focusing on all the positive things the father of my children does and can't help but be thankful. I'm beyond blessed with our children and also with Todd, who treasures being a daddy.

DARE TO PAIR

Toast your man tonight with the dapper bottle of **Francis Ford Coppola Diamond Collection Black Label Claret**. This suave red wine is layered with flavors of blackberry, cassis, and roasted espresso. The presentation alone will illustrate the many thanks you have for that class act man o' yours.

Being a Baseball Family

What is baseball-mom fever to me? It's that I just can't get enough—the cheering, the butterflies, the hot days in the sun, sunflower seeds, big-league chew, the smell of summer. It's the crack of the bat and the pop of the mitt while the kids are running around playing as their big brothers are balling it up. It's good calls, bad calls, homeruns, triples, doubles, base hits. Then there are the friendships you make with people you now call family, funny pictures, good music, nights in hotels, kids in the pool, and team bonding. But, most of all, it's making lasting memories with my boys, my family, and my baseball family—time I wouldn't trade for *anything* in the world.

This hasn't always been the case. I grew up in a house full of girls. To my surprise, I had three boys, was a little bit out of sorts about it, yet I had *no* idea what I was in for.

My oldest son Blake started playing T-ball when he was five. Where we live, we all know this means many cold days and nights in the howling spring wind. I just kept asking myself: when will this be over? But, he loved the game and kept at it. Nights are long when you're standing out in the cold trying to watch games with a new baby. But it didn't take long before the game started to really pick up with the kids making actual plays. All of a sudden it hit me and I didn't even see it coming: baseball-mom *fever*.

Blake was nominated for the all-star team so we started spending summers traveling to tournaments. It was a whole new way of life. Again I had no idea where this road would take us as a family. But by then, we *all* had the fever. My husband Rick started coaching and has been coaching our boys ever since. By the time Blake was 11, his team had taken second at state. And they went on to win the state championship two years in a row so they were on their way to regionals.

In the meantime, my middle son, Hunter, was nine and also in love with the game. His all-star team won at state and then became the State Champions in their division. If you know little league at all, you know how rare it is for two brothers to win the State Championship in the same season. Once again, we headed to regionals, where both of my sons' teams did well and made it to the semifinals.

Blake was fortunate to spend 10 days in Japan playing baseball. The boys stayed with host families, went sightseeing and had many interesting experiences while they were there. Meanwhile, Hunter's second-place team was invited to regionals by the commissioner of our region. So on the same day that I sent thirteen-year-old Blake off to Japan, I set out traveling to regionals with Hunter.

At this point, my youngest son Preston developed a love for the game that's all his *own*. So I can now officially say that I have a *baseball* family and I'm a baseball mom. I wash uniforms, scrub pants, pack coolers, make lunch at the fields and dinner in the hotel. I'm the official scorekeeper, making sure coach and team have what they need, and the unofficial secretary, sending group texts to everyone. I plan team dinners, keep the peace (very important), and love every second of it. If my husband didn't coach, I honestly wouldn't know what to do with myself.

I had no idea that a sport could bring me to where I love a game as much as my kids and husband do. It may be in a different way and for different reasons, but it all fits together. I also love all of the people involved, the other families, and every kid on the teams as if they were my own. We truly are one big family that travels together and would have each other's backs at any time! I didn't grow up experiencing any of this as a kid. I think that my children are pretty lucky to have had this experience.

My family breathes baseball. It's truly the glue that holds us together at times. I would never trade the memories I have of my sons making plays and hitting homeruns for anything. Now Hunter's 12th season is winding down and though my heart feels heavy at times that we might not know summers like these in the future, I look forward to all that we have ahead of us as a family and to the many *more* memories we will make. But baseball and its summers will forever be in my heart.

DARE TO PAIR

Becoming a baseball family is only one of the ways to make memories and cherish being a family. Whether it's summer yet or not, celebrate what summer means to your family by holding up a glass (or, as in this story, Nalgene bottle) of this delicious wine: **Playtime Blonde**. Containing ripe, tropical fruits, citrus, and golden apple it will remind you of all the golden summers, past, present and future.

I Didn't Expect to Find Love Again

I knew I was tempting fate by splitting from my husband when I was 31, without a firm job and with two young children to raise. While there was no doubt I would be able to succeed on my own; I just didn't know how I would actually *feel* on my own. I loved independence and doing my own thing, but I also enjoyed having the security of a relationship and someone waiting for me at home. I was taking a huge risk, and everyone knew it.

My friends reminded me: "Girl, there aren't that many men in our town, not reputable, single, well-established men anyway. You're better off working it out." But, I knew I wasn't better off "working it out." In my heart, I knew that, even though I may never fall in love or get married again, the opportunity to meet and date men was definitely there simply because men had always paid attention to me.

Once I filed for divorce, I swore to myself that marriage wasn't for me. Though I'd likely find a companion, I was pretty sure marriage wasn't in the cards for me again. When my husband and I were separated and divorcing, I talked to a few different guys. I wasn't exactly sure how to go about the dating thing, but I knew I wanted to have a little fun. Solely focused on making my husband and children happy since I was 23-years-old, I was ready for the new phase in my life.

Having found an excellent job, I learned how to balance being a mom when my kids were with me and to focus on being a successful career woman when they weren't. My job paid me enough to be comfortable on my own, yet afforded me the time to focus on my passion, writing. When I got a book deal mere months after divorcing, I realized the sky was truly the limit—if even that. Hey, didn't men land on the moon? Just sayin'.

Soon after my split, one of the guys I talked to surprisingly stole my attention completely. He was someone I maybe wouldn't have paid too much attention to before, mostly because he wasn't my type. A teacher at my daughter's school, I saw him daily, but didn't take too much notice of him at first. Yet then I started to realize that his daily waves hello came with true stares of curiosity.

Meanwhile, one of my friends asked me if I'd talked to the "cute phys ed teacher" yet. As the weeks went by, it became clear as his smiles and waves grew bigger that he was interested. I had no idea how complicated it would become. He friended me on Facebook one day. I didn't even know his name, so I had to look at his Facebook page to see who this dude was. Sure enough, it *was* my daughters phys ed teacher. I called my friend to see if that was weird. Do I friend him back? What if he gets the wrong impression? If I don't friend him back, will it be weird to see him every day? So I friended him back, deciding it was the safer of the two choices—and it became one of the best decisions I'd ever made.

Then he wrote me with the excuse of why he friended me in the first place. He thought I was nice, I always waved at school, yada yada. I kept the conversation minimal, one sentence answers so he'd know I was *not* interested. But I secretly was. During the whole e-mail and phone phase, he was persistent, saying and doing all the right things at all the right times. When I blew him off, he kept in touch, but gave me enough space so I wasn't annoyed. When I finally went crazy and told him about all the issues in my life, he listened and gave me advice.

The first time we met, I was nervous. Not knowing where this was headed, I just knew the attention felt good and I really enjoyed talking to him. We briefly met in town just before I was leaving for a trip. He grabbed my hand, and I felt the nervous butterflies of doing something I wasn't supposed to do. I needed *time*, more time. Even though I told him I wasn't ready for him to kiss me, he did anyway. And he was the most amazing kisser. I didn't want it to stop, but I pushed him away and ran for my car. I knew I was in trouble—there was no going back now.

It all made me feel guilty and out of place. I cared about this guy, but I was going through a pretty traumatic divorce, with two young kids in the midst of it. How could I throw a new relationship into that landmine? I thought I needed an appropriate amount of time to be on my own and truly assumed that I'd never be in a serious relationship, maybe ever, again. But, each time I tried to pull away from him, there was a magnetic force that pulled us back together. I couldn't stay away from him, no matter how hard I tried.

Over time, we became close friends. He was also going through a bad breakup. We both had complications with our exes and houses that wouldn't be resolved quickly. I was becoming more interested in him, but I was hesitant. Wasn't I supposed to sow my wild oats and enjoy being on my own now that I was single again?

After a few months, I *officially* introduced him to my kids. Obviously, he'd known them both from school, but it was different to meet someone outside of the school context. I was the most nervous about this than anything. What if they hated him? What if they were mad because I'd taken *away* their teacher? What if he thought they were too rambunctious? What if we all didn't mesh? I was a wreck. All this and more swirled through my head. How does anyone date with kids?!

He was wonderful: patient, loving, kind, giving. He was everything every single girl I've ever talked to could want in a new man. I finally *had* it. I hadn't even been looking, and there it was.

In the past year, every single thing you could imagine might come between us happened. His ex. My ex. Some of our friends. I have to give it to the people who stood beside me and supported this new and unexpected development in my life. Some people weren't so supportive, and things got nasty. On several occasions, I thought: that's it, I *give!* This *can't* be worth this struggle. But it was and it still *is.* And no matter what happens down the road, I will treasure this experience as a learning lesson and time in my life that won't be forgotten.

We may not be the American picture of a perfect family, but, together, we are working on our own picture of perfect. While I didn't plan on having a serious relationship so soon after splitting from my husband of eight years, I'm thankful it found me. I'm happy I was weak enough to be open to it and let it happen because now—I'm truly *happy*.

As I watch myself heal, learn, and love in this brave new world, I also watch my children reflect my new happiness—they're thriving. Divorced with kids is not the end of the road. For some, it may just be the beginning.

DARE TO PAIR

Divorce can knock any hot mom off her heels. Before you completely give up on relationship, slip on that cute, little black number and indulge in some of this deep maroon **Little Black Dress Merlot**. With aromas of sweet black cherries and soft vanilla, just as the hint of plum hits your taste buds, you'll be reminded that *you still got it, girl.*

We Had the Best Summer *Ever*

This past summer, we were constantly on the go, spending time with friends at impromptu pool parties and neighborhood gatherings. Sleeping late. Going to movies. Gluttonous eating and drinking. And now it's over. I feel like it was yanked out from under us right in the midst of the fun and frivolity. And yet, it has to end, doesn't it? Life has to continue to move forward. My kids have to go back to school and become educated, productive members of society. I have to stop barreling toward 300 pounds with the way I've been devouring food and drink. We all have to get back to "normal." Normal totally *blows*.

Not really. It's just that we're coming off of such a nice summer. The kids and I really spent almost all day every day together. There was never much of an agenda, yet our days always seemed to be filled. One of my favorite things was that we started a new tradition of walking in the neighborhood at night and just talking, relating to one another. It was the one time in the day when the girls didn't get on each other's nerves. We laughed and acted silly and occasionally ran into other neighborhood friends. The girls' favorite thing to do on our walks was play "Would You Rather." We would ask each other hard-hitting questions like, "Would you rather teetee in your pants or throw up on your teacher on the first day of school?" Then we would each explain why we chose the choice we did. Utter ridiculousness. But it was such fun.

We travelled some, mostly to the lake, and many times with friends. People coming to the lake house is a great way to reconnect with friends we don't often see. I especially enjoyed watching our kids become friends with our friends' kids. Even though they may only see each other at the lake once a year, they look forward to it and fall right back in line every time. It was nice. One day, we invited all the neighborhood moms and their kids over. There were 22 of us there—good heavens, what were we thinking?! But, it was an absolute blast!

We also went to Chicago—the girls' first plane ride! They were so cute rolling their suitcases through the airport. They acted as though they felt so big when they were served peanuts and Sprite on the plane. It never occurred to them to be afraid of any of it. I wish I had flown at their age; I've always been very nervous to fly, sweaty palms and all. But they just sat back and enjoyed the view. They also had a blast once we got to the city. The fact that we took them to a two-story American Girl store helped, I'm sure.

As the first-day-of-school date approached, I was feeling

very sad and more aware than ever of the time we couldn't get back—time to sneak off to the pool or to the movies or just out to lunch. The older we get, the faster time seems to go by.

Summer days like this past one are the good times; they are the days we will remember. I miss them so much even though, admittedly, it's nice to be back on a schedule. Soon enough we will all be in the thick of the school year and fall festivities as last summer becomes a lovely memory. But in the years ahead, when I talk with my kids about the beautiful moments in my life, it will be the summer I recall most fondly.

DARE TO PAIR

The end of summer is always so bittersweet, but you don't have to bid it adieu just yet. The medium-bodied, complex **Flip Flop Riesling**, with peach, apricot, and melon, leads to a satisfying, smooth finish. Tropical notes and sweet aromas will bring you to a place where memories of summer are wafting through your mind.

Trusting Yourself

Listen to your heart.

It may sound cliché, but there are times in my life that I have wished I'd listened closer. This is why it is the main piece of advice I hope sticks with my children through the years. It's all encompassing, I think. Whatever the choices that need to be made—about the lovers in your life, the clothes you wear, the direction of your studies and career—from the smallest to the largest decisions you may ever face, *listen to your heart.*

Life can be so confusing. Your family and friends, teachers, community and even the media are all trying to convince you of what to do. But, nobody knows you more than, well, *you.* Even once you do figure yourself out, your confidence may be fleeting so it can be hard to see that you *truly* can stand out and be someone special, someone unique, someone amazing.

I was watching the LEGO movie with my boys a few nights ago and I fell in love with something the character Emmet said:

"You are the most talented, most interesting, and most extraordinary person in the universe. And you are *capable of amazing things.* Because you are special. And so am I. And so is everyone."

What does this message have to do with listening to your heart? I think that, deep down, under that annoying, insistent voice that is always telling you that you *can't* do something, is the real you trying to convince you of what you *should* be doing. There is a quote by Vincent Van Gogh I just saw on a friend's Facebook page that excited me:

"If you hear a voice within you say 'you cannot paint,' then by all means paint, and that voice will be silenced."

How perfectly brilliant! Isn't it just at the moment we've convinced ourselves that we can't do something when we most need to hold on and persevere? This is when we most need to listen to that special voice inside, the one that cheers for us to push forward and become the person we want to be. If you quiet the chattering in your head, you can hear your heart's destiny.

While my children are still young, I plan on being better at helping them to follow their hearts as well—whether it's sup-porting a crazy mismatched style or an interest in subjects of which I don't approve. I also want to show them how to be their own persons by the example of my actions—by not suc-cumbing to peer pressure (have another glass of wine! stay for another hour!) or agreeing with someone's opinion, even when I know I feel differently. It could be as simple as wearing a T-shirt I love that may not be in style or changing careers to one I know is right for me despite what others think. I want to be a reflection of the beauty of listening, listening to your heart and being who you truly are meant to be. Because that, moms, is the best lesson we can teach our children.

DARE TO PAIR

You've got a heart of gold, my friend. Listen to it closely. The very mellow flavors of **Ciccone Vineyards Vino di Oro** table wine will remind you to celebrate the beauty in *you*. This semi-sweet white wine exhibits grapefruit aromas with apricot, floral, and citrus flavors and is oh, so *soothing*. Toast yourself and the wonderful mom you truly are!

Wine Index

REDS

Note: When name of winery is not part of the wine name, it follows the name

REDS *(cont.)*

Wine Index

Note: When name of winery is not part of the wine name, it follows the name

WHITES

Note: When name of winery is not part of the wine name, it follows the name